Chocolate

Chocolate

70 of the best recipes

hamlyn

A Pyramid Paperback

First published in Great Britain in 2007 by Hamlyn,
a division of Octopus Publishing Group Ltd,
2–4 Heron Quays, London E14 4JP

The material in this book has appeared in the
following books published by Hamlyn: *Kitchen
Library: Baking*; *The Bread Book*; *Chocolate*;
Kitchen Library: Chocolate; *The Christmas Collection*;
Crème Brûlée; *Fairy Cakes*; *15-Minute Feasts*;
Fresh Baked; *Get Sizzling*; *Gourmet Low GI*; *Great
Grilled Sandwiches*; *Martini*, *The Mediterranean
Collection*; *Pancakes*; *Simply Cadbury's Chocolate*;
Soufflés; *Tart*; *30-Minute Italian*; *Viva Italia*

ISBN-13: 978-0-600-61619-1
ISBN-10: 0-600-61619-3

A CIP catalogue record for this book is available
from the British Library

Printed and bound in China

10 9 8 7 6 5 4 3 2 1

Notes
Both metric and imperial measurements have been
given in all recipes. Use one set of measurements
only and not a mixture of both.

Standard level spoon measurements are used in
all recipes.
1 tablespoon = one 15 ml spoon
1 teaspoon = one 5 ml spoon

This book includes dishes made with nuts and
nut derivatives. It is advisable for those with known
allergic reactions to nuts and nut derivatives and
those who may be potentially vulnerable to these
allergies, such as pregnant and nursing mothers,
invalids, the elderly, babies and children, to avoid
dishes made with nuts and nut oils. It is also prudent
to check the labels of pre-prepared ingredients for
the possible inclusion of nut derivatives.

The Department of Health advises that eggs should
not be consumed raw. This book contains some
dishes made with raw or lightly cooked eggs.
It is prudent for more vulnerable people, such as
pregnant and nursing mothers, invalids, the elderly,
babies and young children, to avoid uncooked or
lightly cooked dishes made with eggs.

Contents

Introduction

Since its introduction to Europe several centuries ago, the rich colour, unique texture, tempting aroma and delicious flavour of chocolate have provided us with one of the most irresistible and popular of foods. Whether you are making a few cookies or a large, luscious gâteau, chocolate is the one ingredient guaranteed to set your tastebuds quivering with anticipation.

The chocolate we enjoy today has been refined and improved out of all recognition since it was first discovered by the Maya, an ancient people who inhabited Central America. The Maya used cocoa beans not only to make a cold drink called *chocolatl*, but also as a form of currency. In this way the secret of *chocolatl* was passed to the Aztecs of Mexico, who valued it so highly that it is said the Spanish conquistador Hernando Cortés was served *chocolatl* mixed with ground maize and flavoured with vanilla and chillies in a golden goblet at the court of the Emperor Montezuma.

Chocolate arrived in Europe in the 1520s, soon after the Spanish had conquered Mexico, and the European version, which reached Britain in the 1650s, was an expensive luxury, by now served hot and without the chillies and sold at the newly established London chocolate houses. It was not until Victorian times, when processes for making solid blocks of eating chocolate had been perfected, that chocolate was used other than as a drink.

ABOUT CHOCOLATE

The cocoa tree is still grown in Central and South America, although today West Africa is the world's major cocoa producer. A tree produces 20–30 pods a year, each containing 30–40 cocoa beans buried among the soft,

pulpy fibres. The annual crop from one tree is enough to make only 500 g (1 lb) of cocoa. Once harvested, the cocoa beans are fermented, then left to dry before being shipped abroad. When they reach the cocoa-processing factories the beans are cleaned and roasted to develop chocolate's wonderful aroma and flavour. After roasting, the beans undergo various treatments to produce cocoa solids, which are the basic ingredient of all chocolate products, and it is the production process that determines the quality of the chocolate. When you buy plain or milk chocolate remember that the higher the proportion of cocoa solids, the purer the chocolate flavour will be.

TYPES OF CHOCOLATE

There is an increasingly extensive range of chocolate available for both cooking and eating. The darkest plain chocolate contains 80 per cent or more cocoa solids and has an intensely chocolaty (though not necessarily bitter) flavour because of its lower sugar content. Perfect for those who prefer a less sweet, richer flavour, it's also the best for use in savoury chocolate recipes.

Slightly sweeter is plain chocolate that contains 60-70 per cent cocoa solids. This has a dense, chocolaty flavour and is a good all-rounder, ideal for recipes in this book that are made with ordinary dark chocolate. This type of chocolate melts well to a smooth, glossy texture and retains its full flavour. Less expensive brands of plain chocolate contain 30–40 per cent cocoa solids. These are acceptable in family puddings and cakes, but you might like to splash out on the purer chocolate for special occasions.

Milk chocolate is considerably sweeter than plain chocolate and has added milk, sugar and flavourings, such as vanilla. It contains 20–30 per cent cocoa solids. Again, use the percentage of cocoa solids as a guide when you are buying.

White chocolate contains no solids. Instead, it is made with cocoa butter (the edible fat that is extracted from the beans during processing) and milk, sugar and flavouring.

Cocoa powder, a by-product of the processing method, has a strong, bitter flavour. Good for intensifying the flavour of chocolate, it should always be cooked and needs additional sweetening.

Never use chocolate-flavoured cake covering. This is usually sold alongside the baking products in supermarkets, but it's an imitation chocolate-flavoured bar of sugar, vegetable oils and flavourings.

Working with chocolate

Success in using chocolate, particularly for decorative cakes and desserts, requires an understanding of the unique qualities of chocolate when it is melted or shaped.

MELTING CHOCOLATE

Melting chocolate is quite easy as long as you take time and care. Plain chocolate is easier to melt than milk chocolate as it has a lower fat content and burns less easily, but gentle heat and minimal stirring are essential in both cases.

On the hob

Break the chocolate into pieces and put them in a heatproof bowl. Rest the bowl over a pan of very gently simmering water, making sure that the base of the bowl cannot come in contact with the water. Once the chocolate starts to melt, turn off the heat and leave it until it is completely melted, stirring once or twice until no lumps remain. Do not over-stir or you might destroy the delicate balance of colour, flavour and texture. It's crucial that no water – steam from the pan, for example – gets into the bowl while the chocolate is melting as this will make the chocolate solidify. When you are pouring the melted chocolate on to paper to make decorations, wipe the bowl base with a cloth as soon as you take it from the heat so that no condensed steam drips into the chocolate. Use the melted chocolate immediately. It will remain soft if you keep it in a warm place while you are working with it.

In the microwave

Use a microwave-proof bowl and melt the chocolate on medium power in one-minute spurts, checking frequently.

In the oven

Put the chocolate in a small ovenproof bowl or dish and leave the bowl in a low oven, 110°C (225°F), Gas Mark ¼, checking frequently. Alternatively, put it in an oven that's been switched off after being used for baking.

With other ingredients

Butter, cream, milk, liqueur or water can be melted with chocolate. Because of the high fat or sugar content of butter and liqueur, the melting time will be reduced.

EQUIPMENT

Little special equipment is required and you will probably already have most of the basic items: large and small heavy-based saucepans, hand mixers, whisks, knives and brushes. The following items are especially useful.

Bowls

You can never have too many bowls. Some recipes require several. Chocolate is usually melted in a small, preferably heatproof glass bowl that fits snugly over a saucepan. Remember that you don't want the bowl to

sink so far into the pan that its base touches the water, but nor do you want it to be so big that it's balanced precariously on top of the pan. In most of the recipes in this book, the melted chocolate is added to other ingredients, so a small bowl will suffice.

Palette knives

These are essential tools for achieving a smooth, even coverage of icing or ganache. You'll need both large and small knives, depending on the size of the cake. They are also useful for spreading melted chocolate thinly on paper to make decorations.

Cool surface

A marble slab is the best surface for setting chocolate caraque and other chocolate decorations. A small one that's not too heavy is ideal, because you can put it in the refrigerator to speed up setting. If you haven't got a marble slab and need an alternative firm surface that can be put in the refrigerator, use a thoroughly clean wooden chopping board (preferably one kept for fruit and sweet dishes) or a thick plate or glass board or tray.

Dipping fork

Use a long, thin-pronged fork for dipping fruits and sweets into chocolate. The chocolate will drip back into the bowl instead of clogging up the tines.

Metal moulds

Small metal moulds are perfect for individual portions of puddings and desserts and are used in several recipes in this book. Traditional pudding-shaped moulds have a capacity of 150 ml (¼ pint), and the slightly smaller,

straight-sided dariole moulds have a capacity of 125 ml (4 fl oz). Bear in mind that rich desserts are often better in smaller moulds.

Piping bags

Paper or cloth piping bags are used for piping scribbled decorations directly on to cakes and desserts or on to paper for setting. To make a disposable paper bag, fold a 25 cm (10 inch) square of greaseproof paper or nonstick baking paper diagonally in half to make a triangle. Cut along the folded line. Holding the long edge towards you, curl the right-hand point of the triangle over to meet the centre point, forming a cone. Then bring the left-hand point over the cone so that the three points meet. Fold the paper over several times at the points to stop it unravelling. Half-fill the bag with melted chocolate and fold down the open end to secure the bag before snipping off the tip. Test the flow and snip off a little more for a thicker flow. If the chocolate sets in the bag, pop it briefly into the microwave until softened.

If you don't want to use a piping bag, you can still achieve effective finishes by drizzling melted chocolate from a teaspoon.

Using chocolate

Chocolate can be grated, curled, scribbled or melted and modelled into almost any shape. Some techniques take a matter of minutes, while other, more imaginative, sculptural forms (such as the cases on page 64) require a little extra patience and planning. These decorations will provide the perfect finishing touch for your special chocolate desserts and gâteaux. You can make chocolate decorations up to a week in advance and store them in an airtight container in a cool place.

If you find that the chocolate is brittle and crumbles when you attempt to grate it or try to make decorations such as chocolate curls or caraque, it may be too cold. If you think this is the case, try leaving the chocolate to warm up for a while at room temperature or give it a very quick blast in the microwave to soften it slightly.

GRATED CHOCOLATE
Scattering some coarsely grated plain, milk or white chocolate over creamy desserts, ice creams and chilled drinks will make them look really appealing.

CHOCOLATE CURLS
Use a swivel-bladed potato peeler to pare off thick curls from the smooth side of a bar of chocolate and scatter them over cheesecakes, ice cream, trifles, cakes and chocolate mousses. The chunkier the bar, the larger the curls will be. If the curls are very small, microwave the chocolate in 15-second bursts until it softens or leave it for a while at room temperature to warm up before use.

CHOCOLATE CARAQUE
These professional-looking curls take a little more effort but are well worth making for a special cake or dessert. They will keep well in the refrigerator for several weeks or in the freezer for longer.

Spread melted chocolate in a thin layer on a marble slab or a clean, smooth surface, such as a new, plastic chopping board or sturdy baking sheet. Leave to set. Holding a fine-

DOUBLE CHOCOLATE SHAVINGS

Melt 150 g (5 oz) white chocolate with 25 g (1 oz) unsalted butter and turn into the tub as above. Melt 150 g (5 oz) plain or milk chocolate with 25 g (1 oz) unsalted butter and spoon the mix over the white chocolate. Leave to set, then shape as above.

CHOCOLATE LEAVES

Firm but flexible leaves, such as fresh bay or rose leaves, are best for making decorations for festive desserts and chocolate logs. Wash and dry the leaves well, then brush or spoon a little chocolate on to the underside. Leave to set, then gently peel away the leaves.

JAGGED CHOCOLATE BRITTLE

To make chocolate brittle, spread melted chocolate on to a tray or baking sheet lined with baking paper. Scatter finely chopped toasted nuts (if liked) over the chocolate and chill until the chocolate is really brittle, then peel away the paper and snap the chocolate into jagged shards. These can be speared into chocolate desserts and special-occasion cakes.

bladed knife at a 45-degree angle, draw it across the chocolate so that you scrape off curls. If the chocolate is too soft and doesn't curl, pop it in the refrigerator for a few minutes. If it is brittle and breaks off in thin shards, leave it at room temperature for a while or put it very briefly in the microwave before trying again.

CHOCOLATE SHAVINGS

To make elaborate curls for special cakes and desserts, melt 300 g (10 oz) plain or white chocolate with 25 g (1 oz) unsalted butter. Turn the mixture into a clean 250 g (8 oz) butter or margarine tub or another similar-sized container, and leave until the chocolate is set but not brittle. Then press the chocolate out of the tub and pare off shavings. As you work, protect the end of the slab with foil to prevent the heat of your hand from melting the chocolate.

CHOCOLATE RIBBONS

Cut out some 15 x 3 cm (6 x 1¼ inch) strips of nonstick baking paper. Spread melted chocolate over the strips, taking it almost as far as the edges of the baking paper. Arrange 4–6 small wooden spoons, pens or chunky pencils in a row on a small tray, spacing them slightly apart from each other. Then carefully lift the chocolate-covered strips and lower them over the spoons. Leave the chocolate strips to set in ribbony waves. When you are sure that the chocolate has set, gently peel away the paper.

CHOCOLATE SCRIBBLES

Line a tray with nonstick baking paper. Fill a paper piping bag with a little melted chocolate and snip off the merest tip. 'Draw' shapes on the paper – scribbled lines, curvy swirls or filigree patterns – and leave them to set. Peel the paper away and use the scribbles to decorate chilled desserts. Don't make the patterns too delicate or they will break.

CHOCOLATE-DIPPED FRUITS

Dipping in chocolate is great for fruit, such as strawberries, cherries, physalis, banana chunks or dates. Half-dip the fruit into melted chocolate, let the excess drip off and place the fruit on a sheet of nonstick baking paper until set. This technique can also be used for chocolate fudge, truffles or nuts.

CUT-OUTS

Use small biscuit or cake cutters, which are available from specialist shops, to make shapes for decorating cakes and desserts. Spread melted chocolate on a tray lined with nonstick baking paper. Leave it to set, then press out the shapes with the cutters.

Basic recipes

Glossy chocolate sauce

Preparation time **5 minutes**,
  plus cooling
Cooking time **3 minutes**
Serves **6**

125 g (4 oz) caster sugar
125 ml (4 fl oz) water
200 g (7 oz) plain dark chocolate,
  chopped
25 g (1 oz) unsalted butter

1 Put the sugar and water in a small, heavy-based saucepan. Cook, stirring the mixture constantly with a wooden spoon, over a low heat until the sugar has completely dissolved.

2 Bring to the boil and boil for 1 minute, then leave to cool for a further minute. Add the chocolate and butter and leave until both have melted.

3 Stir until smooth and glossy, returning to a gentle heat if the last of the chocolate doesn't melt completely.

Ganache

Preparation time **5 minutes**,
  plus cooling
Cooking time **3 minutes**
Makes **sufficient to
  cover a 20 cm (8 inch)
  chocolate cake**

300 ml (½ pint) double cream
300 g (10 oz) plain dark chocolate,
  chopped

1 Heat the cream in a medium-sized, heavy-based saucepan until it is bubbling around the edges. Remove from the heat and add the chocolate.

2 Leave to stand for a few minutes until the chocolate has melted, then stir well and turn the mixture into a clean bowl.

3 Chill until the mixture holds its shape when stirred; this should take 15–45 minutes.

Fudge icing

Preparation time **10 minutes**
Cooking time **10 minutes**
Makes **sufficient to sandwich
and cover the top of an
18–20 cm (7–8 inch) cake**

150 g (5 oz) plain dark chocolate,
chopped
150 ml (¼ pint) double cream
125 g (4 oz) light muscovado sugar
65 g (2½ oz) unsalted butter
1 teaspoon vanilla extract

1 Melt the chocolate in a small bowl. Put the cream and sugar in a medium-sized, heavy-based saucepan and stir gently until the sugar has dissolved.

2 Bring the cream mixture to the boil and simmer, without stirring, for about 4 minutes until it is bubbling vigorously and has become thickened and caramely.

3 Remove the mixture from the heat and stir in the butter until it has melted.

4 Add the melted chocolate and vanilla extract and turn the icing into a bowl. Cool, then chill for about 30 minutes until the mixture is thickened and spreadable. If it becomes solid in the refrigerator leave it at room temperature for a while or soften it carefully in the microwave.

Crisp chocolate pastry

Preparation time **10 minutes**

Makes **sufficient to line a 20–23 cm (8–9 inch) pastry case**

15 g (½ oz) cocoa powder
125 g (4 oz) plain flour
25 g (1 oz) icing sugar
75 g (3 oz) lightly salted butter, diced
1 egg yolk

1 Sift the cocoa powder, flour and icing sugar into a bowl. Add the butter and rub it in with the fingertips until the mixture resembles fine breadcrumbs.

2 Add the egg yolk and 1 teaspoon cold water and mix to a dough. Alternatively, blend the butter into the flour mixture in a food processor, then blend in the egg yolk and water until the mixture binds together.

3 Turn the dough on to a lightly floured surface and knead lightly until smooth. Wrap and chill for at least 30 minutes before using.

4 Put a greased flan ring or tin on a baking sheet. Roll out the pastry so that it is about 5 cm (2 inches) larger all round than the diameter of the ring or tin. Roll the pastry loosely around the rolling pin and lift it over the tin. Carefully unroll the pastry into the tin, gently easing it into the tin and taking care not to stretch it or leave air gaps underneath.

5 Carefully press the pastry into the flutes with your fingers. Turn any surplus pastry outwards from the rim, then roll the rolling pin straight over the top so that the surplus pastry is cut and falls away, leaving a neat edge.

Chocolate crème anglaise

Preparation time **10 minutes**
Cooking time **15 minutes**
Serves **6**

300 ml (½ pint) milk
300 ml (½ pint) single cream
6 egg yolks
25 g (1 oz) caster sugar
1 teaspoon cornflour
75 g (3 oz) plain dark chocolate,
   chopped

1 Put the milk and cream in a medium-sized, heavy-based saucepan and bring slowly to the boil. In a large bowl whisk together the egg yolks, sugar and cornflour.

2 Pour the hot milk and cream over the egg mixture, whisking well. Transfer the mixture to a clean pan.

3 Cook the custard over a gentle heat, stirring constantly with a wooden spoon, for about 10 minutes or until it thickly coats the back of the spoon. Do not let the custard boil or it might curdle.

4 Remove the custard from the heat and stir in the chocolate until it has melted. Serve warm with the pudding of your choice.

Little cakes, cookies and snacks

Hot chocolate pancakes with spiced ricotta and raisins

Preparation time 20 minutes
Cooking time **20–30 minutes**
Serves **4**

Pancakes
100 g (3½ oz) plain flour
15 g (½ oz) cocoa powder
1 egg, beaten
300 ml (½ pint) milk or half and half
   milk and water
oil, for frying

Filling
1 piece of stem ginger, about 15 g
   (½ oz), finely chopped
2 tablespoons caster sugar, plus
   extra for dusting
250 g (8 oz) ricotta cheese
50 g (2 oz) raisins
150 g (5 oz) white chocolate,
   chopped
3 tablespoons double cream

To serve
1 quantity Glossy Chocolate Sauce
   (see page 14)
lightly whipped cream (optional)

1 Make the pancakes. Sieve the flour and cocoa powder into a bowl and make a well in the centre. Add the egg and about half the milk and whisk to incorporate the dry ingredients. Whisk in the remaining milk to make a smooth batter.

2 Heat a little oil in a small, nonstick frying pan and spoon about 2 tablespoons of batter into the pan. Hold the pan at an angle so that the batter covers the base and cook for 1–2 minutes. Turn over with a palette knife and cook briefly. Transfer to greaseproof paper and use the remaining batter to make 8–10 pancakes in total.

3 Make the filling. Mix the ginger in a bowl with the sugar, ricotta, raisins, chocolate and cream. Place spoonfuls of the filling in the centres of the pancakes and fold them into quarters, enclosing the filling.

4 Place the pancakes in a lightly greased, shallow ovenproof dish and dust with sugar. Bake in a preheated oven, 200°C (400°F), Gas Mark 6, for 10 minutes or until heated through. Serve hot with the glossy chocolate sauce and cream, if liked.

Fruit and nut cinnamon filos

Preparation time **10 minutes**, plus chilling
Cooking time **about 4 minutes**
Serves **4**

200 g (7 oz) fruit and nut chocolate bar
8 sheets filo pastry
1 egg, beaten
40 g (1½ oz) caster sugar
1 teaspoon ground cinnamon
oil, for deep frying
roughly chopped toasted hazelnuts or almonds, to decorate

1 Use a warm knife to cut the chocolate bar widthways into 16 sticks. Lay one sheet of pastry on the work surface and brush with a little beaten egg. Cover with another sheet and brush with more egg. Cut the sheets into 4 rectangles.

2 Place a stick of chocolate on one rectangle of pastry. Fold the 2 short ends over the ends of the chocolate and brush with more egg. Roll up the pastry so the chocolate is enclosed. Shape the remainder in the same way. Chill for 30 minutes.

3 Mix together the caster sugar and cinnamon. Heat the oil to a depth of 5 cm (2 inch) in a large saucepan to 180–190°C (350–375°F) or until a cube of bread browns in 30 seconds.

4 Add half the pastries and fry for about 2 minutes or until golden. Drain on kitchen paper and cook the remainder of the pastries in the same way. Toss the pastries in the cinnamon sugar and serve scattered with the toasted nuts.

White chocolate and raspberry puffs

Preparation time **20 minutes**,
plus chilling
Cooking time **15 minutes**
Serves **6**

350 g (12 oz) puff pastry (thawed
if frozen)
150 g (5 oz) raspberries
icing sugar, for dusting

White chocolate cream
200 ml (7 fl oz) single cream
½ vanilla pod
200 g (7 oz) white chocolate,
chopped

1 Roll out the pastry on a lightly floured surface until it forms a rectangle 2 mm (⅛ inch) thick. Cut the pastry into 6 rectangles, each 7 x 12 cm (3 x 5 inches), and put them on a baking sheet. Chill for 30 minutes. Bake in a preheated oven, 200°C (400°F), Gas Mark 6, for 15 minutes or until the pastry is puffed and golden. Transfer to a wire rack to cool.

2 Make the chocolate cream. Put the cream and vanilla pod in a heavy-based saucepan and heat gently until it reaches boiling point. Remove from the heat and scrape the seeds from the vanilla pod into the cream (discard the pod). Immediately stir in the chocolate and continue stirring until it has melted. Allow to cool, chill for 1 hour until firm and then whisk until stiff.

3 Split the pastries in half crossways and fill each with white chocolate cream and raspberries. Serve dusted with icing sugar.

Caramel pine nut slices

Preparation time **20 minutes**,
plus chilling and cooling
Cooking time **25–30 minutes**
Serves **12**

125 g (4 oz) unsalted butter,
    softened
65 g (2½ oz) caster sugar, plus extra
    for dusting
125 g (4 oz) plain flour
65 g (2½ oz) rice flour
pinch of salt
200 g (7 oz) plain dark chocolate,
    chopped

Pine nut caramel
50 g (2 oz) unsalted butter
50 g (2 oz) soft brown sugar
395 g (12¾ oz) can sweetened
    condensed milk
50 g (2 oz) pine nuts

1 Put the butter and sugar in a bowl and beat until light and smooth. Sift in the flour, rice flour and salt and work the ingredients together to form a soft dough. Shape the dough into a flat disc, wrap it in clingfilm and chill for 30 minutes.

2 Lightly oil a 20 cm (8 inch) square baking tin and line it with baking paper, allowing the paper to overhang the sides of the tin. Roll out the dough on a lightly floured surface and press it into the prepared tin, smoothing it as flat as possible. Bake in a preheated oven, 190°C (375°F), Gas Mark 5, for 20-25 minutes or until golden. Remove from the oven and leave to cool.

3 Make the pine nut caramel. Put the butter, sugar and condensed milk in a saucepan and heat gently, stirring constantly, until the butter has melted and the sugar has completely dissolved. Increase the heat and bring to the boil, whisking constantly for up to 5 minutes until the mixture thickens. Remove from the heat, stir in the pine nuts and pour the mixture over the shortbread layer. Leave until set. Chill for 2 hours or until really firm.

4 Put the chocolate in a bowl set over a pan of gently simmering water and stir until the chocolate has melted. Pour it over the caramel layer, smoothing it flat with a palette knife. Leave to set, remove from the tin and cut the mixture into fingers.

White chocolate curl cakes

Preparation time **35 minutes**
Cooking time **20 minutes**
Makes **12 cakes**

175 g (6 oz) unsalted butter,
    softened
125 g (4 oz) caster sugar
125 g (4 oz) self-raising flour
3 eggs
125 g (4 oz) ground almonds
    or hazelnuts
50 g (2 oz) unblanched hazelnuts,
    coarsely chopped and toasted
175 g (6 oz) white chocolate chips
100 g (3½ oz) white chocolate bar
1 quantity Fudge Icing made with
    white chocolate (see page 15)
icing sugar, for dusting

1 Put the butter, sugar, flour, eggs and ground almonds or hazelnuts in a bowl and beat until pale and creamy. Reserve a handful of chopped hazelnuts for decoration and add the remainder to the creamed mixture with the chocolate chips. Mix to combine.

2 Line a 12-section muffin tin with paper cases and spoon the mixture into the cases. Bake in a preheated oven, 180°C (350°F), Gas Mark 4, for about 20 minutes or until they are risen and just firm to the touch. Transfer to a wire rack to cool.

3 Use a vegetable peeler to pare off curls from the chocolate bar. Set the chocolate curls aside in a cool place while you ice the cakes.

4 Use a small palette knife to spread the fudge icing all over the tops of the cakes. Pile the chocolate curls on top and lightly dust with icing sugar.

Mocha cupcakes

Preparation time **15 minutes**,
 plus cooling
Cooking time **30 minutes**
Makes **12 cakes**

250 ml (8 fl oz) water
250 g (8 oz) caster sugar
125 g (4 oz) unsalted butter
2 tablespoons cocoa powder, sifted
1/2 teaspoon bicarbonate of soda
2 tablespoons coffee granules
225 g (7 1/2 oz) self-raising flour
2 eggs, lightly beaten
12 chocolate-covered coffee beans,
 to decorate

Icing
150 g (5 oz) plain dark chocolate,
 chopped
150 g (5 oz) unsalted butter, diced
2 tablespoons golden syrup

1 Put the water and sugar in a heavy-based saucepan and heat gently, stirring, until the sugar has dissolved. Stir in the butter, cocoa powder, bicarbonate of soda and coffee granules and bring to the boil, simmer for 5 minutes, remove from the heat and set aside to cool.

2 Beat the flour and eggs into the cooled chocolate mixture until smooth. Line a 12-section muffin tin with paper cases, divide the mixture among the cases and bake in a preheated oven, 180°C (350°F), Gas Mark 4, for 20 minutes or until risen and firm. Cool on a wire rack.

3 Make the icing. Put the chocolate, butter and syrup in a bowl set over a pan of gently simmering water and stir until melted. Remove from the heat and leave to cool to room temperature, then chill until thickened. Spread over the cupcakes, top each with a chocolate coffee bean and leave to set.

Chocolate orange and oatmeal muffins

Preparation time **10 minutes**
Cooking time **15–20 minutes**
Makes **9–10 muffins**

225 g (7½ oz) plain flour
2 teaspoons baking powder
finely grated rind of 1 orange
50 g (2 oz) medium oatmeal
75 g (3 oz) light muscovado sugar
200 g (7 oz) Greek yogurt
4 tablespoons vegetable oil
150 ml (¼ pint) milk
1 egg
200 g (7 oz) milk chocolate,
    chopped
oatmeal, for sprinkling

1 Sift the flour and baking powder into a bowl. Stir in the orange rind, oatmeal and sugar.

2 Beat the yogurt together with the oil, milk and egg and add the mixture to the bowl of dry ingredients with the pieces of chocolate. Use a large metal spoon to fold the ingredients until they are only just combined, adding a little extra milk if the mixture seems dry.

3 Line a 10-section deep muffin tin with paper cases. Divide the mixture among the cases and sprinkle some extra oatmeal over the top. Bake the muffins in a preheated oven, 200°C (400°F), Gas Mark 6, for 15–20 minutes or until risen and just firm. Serve the muffins warm or cold.

Chunky chocolate brownies

Preparation time **20 minutes**
Cooking time **45 minutes**
Makes **18 brownies**

300 g (10 oz) plain dark chocolate,
  chopped
225 g (7½ oz) unsalted butter,
  softened
3 eggs
225 g (7½ oz) light muscovado
  sugar
75 g (3 oz) self-raising flour
175 g (6 oz) walnuts, broken
200 g (7 oz) milk chocolate,
  chopped

1 Melt the plain chocolate in a heavy-based saucepan and stir in the butter.

2 Beat together the eggs and sugar, then beat in the melted plain chocolate mixture. Stir in the flour, walnuts and chopped milk chocolate.

3 Grease and line a shallow 28 x 20 cm (11 x 8 inch) baking tin. Turn the mixture into the prepared tin and level the surface. Bake in a preheated oven, 190°C (375°F), Gas Mark 5, for about 40 minutes until the centre feels just firm on the crust but soft underneath. Take care not to overcook or the brownies will be dry. Leave to cool in the tin. When it is cool, turn out the cake and cut it into 18 squares.

White chocolate biscotti

Preparation time **15 minutes**,
    plus cooling
Cooking time **35 minutes**
Makes **24 biscuits**

300 g (10 oz) white chocolate
25 g (1 oz) unsalted butter, softened
225 g (7½ oz) self-raising flour
50 g (2 oz) light muscovado sugar
2 eggs
1 teaspoon vanilla extract
100 g (3½ oz) pecan nuts, roughly
    chopped
icing sugar, for dusting

1 Chop 100 g (3½ oz) of the chocolate into small pieces
and set aside. Break up the remainder and melt it in a
small bowl with the butter. Leave to cool. Sift the flour
into a mixing bowl and stir in the sugar, eggs, vanilla
extract, nuts and melted chocolate mixture.

2 Add the reserved pieces of chocolate and mix to a
dough. Tip on to a lightly floured surface and halve.

3 Shape each half into a log about 25 cm (10 inches)
long and 2 cm (¾ inch) high. Space well apart on a
lightly oiled baking sheet and bake in a preheated oven,
190°C (375°F), Gas Mark 5, for 18–20 minutes or until
risen, golden and firm. Remove from the oven and
reduce the temperature to 160°C (325°F), Gas Mark 3.

4 Cool the logs for 20 minutes, then cut into 2 cm
(¾ inch) slices. Bake for a further 15 minutes. Dust with
icing sugar and transfer to a wire rack to cool.

Lamingtons

Preparation time **20 minutes**, plus standing
Cooking time **25–30 minutes**
Makes **24 cakes**

125 g (4 oz) unsalted butter, softened
125 g (4 oz) caster sugar
2 eggs, lightly beaten
250 g (8 oz) self-raising flour, sifted
pinch of salt
4 tablespoons milk
1 teaspoon vanilla extract

Icing
400 g (13 oz) icing sugar
100 g (3½ oz) cocoa powder
150–175 ml (5–6 fl oz) boiling water
200 g (7 oz) desiccated coconut

1 Beat the butter and sugar until pale and fluffy. Beat in the eggs, a little at a time. Sift in the flour and salt and fold into the creamed mixture with the milk and vanilla.

2 Oil and base-line a 18 x 25 cm (7 x 10 inch) cake tin and transfer the mixture to the prepared tin. Smooth the surface with a palette knife and bake in a preheated oven, 190°C (375°F), Gas Mark 5, for 25–30 minutes or until risen and firm to the touch. Leave to cool in the tin for 5 minutes and then turn out on to a wire rack to cool. Leave out overnight.

3 Make the icing. Sift the icing sugar and cocoa powder into a bowl, make a well and beat in the boiling water to make a smooth icing with a pouring consistency.

4 Cut the cooled cake into 24 squares. Use 2 forks to dip each cake into the icing and then immediately coat with the coconut. Leave to set on nonstick baking paper.

Chocolate butter biscuits

Preparation time **10 minutes**,
  plus chilling
Cooking time **8–10 minutes**
Makes **36 biscuits**

250 g (8 oz) plain flour
25 g (1 oz) cocoa powder
pinch of salt
200 g (7 oz) chilled unsalted butter,
  diced
100 g (3½ oz) icing sugar
2 egg yolks
1 teaspoon vanilla extract

1 Sift the flour, cocoa powder and salt into a food processor, add the butter and process until the mixture resembles fine breadcrumbs. Add the sugar and pulse briefly, then add the egg yolks and vanilla and process until the mixture just starts to come together.

2 Transfer the dough to a lightly floured work surface and then shape it into a disc. Wrap the dough in clingfilm and chill for 30 minutes.

3 Roll out the dough on a lightly floured surface to 5 mm (¼ inch) thick. Use a 7 cm (3 inch) cutter to stamp out rounds and put them on 3 large, lightly oiled baking sheets. Bake in a preheated oven, 200°C (400°F), Gas Mark 6, for 8–10 minutes or until the biscuits are lightly golden around the edges. Leave them to cool for 5 minutes on the baking sheets and then transfer to a wire rack to cool completely.

Chocolate cinnamon cookies

Preparation time **20 minutes**
Cooking time **15 minutes**
Makes **36 biscuits**

250 g (8 oz) plain flour
2 teaspoons bicarbonate of soda
1 teaspoon ground cinnamon
¼ teaspoon salt
125 g (4 oz) butter, softened
50 g (2 oz) vegetable shortening
275 g (9 oz) sugar
½ teaspoon vanilla extract
1 egg
3 tablespoons golden syrup
50 g (2 oz) plain dark chocolate,
    melted and cooled

1 Sift the flour, bicarbonate of soda, cinnamon and salt into a bowl, then set aside.

2 In a large bowl beat together the butter and shortening. Add 225 g (7½ oz) sugar and beat until fluffy. Add the vanilla extract, then the egg, beating well. Blend in the syrup and chocolate. Gradually work in the dry ingredients, beating until just well combined.

3 Spread the remaining sugar in a shallow tin. Shape the dough into balls, each about 4 cm (1½ inches) across. Place the balls, 6-8 at a time, in the tin and roll in the sugar to coat them lightly all over. Place the balls about 5 cm (2 inches) apart on ungreased baking sheets.

4 Bake in a preheated oven, 180°C (350°F), Gas Mark 4, for about 15 minutes or until firm to the touch. Leave them on the baking sheets for about 2 minutes, then transfer to wire racks to cool completely.

Chocolate kisses

Preparation time **15 minutes**,
plus chilling
Cooking time **15 minutes**
Makes **about 25 kisses**

2 large egg whites
¼ teaspoon cream of tartar
225 g (7½ oz) caster sugar
4 tablespoons cocoa powder, sifted
150 g (5 oz) ground almonds
1 teaspoon almond extract
espresso coffee, to serve

Icing
100 g (3½ oz) plain dark chocolate,
chopped
125 ml (4 fl oz) double cream

1 Whisk the egg whites and cream of tartar in a clean bowl until stiff, then gradually whisk in the sugar, 1 tablespoon at a time, until the mixture thickens. Use a large metal spoon to fold in the cocoa powder, ground almonds and almond extract until evenly combined.

2 Spoon the mixture into a piping bag fitted with a large star nozzle and pipe 2.5 cm (1 inch) rosettes on to 2 large, lined baking sheets (you should have 40–50 rosettes, depending on the size).

3 Bake in a preheated oven, 150°C (300°F), Gas Mark 2, for 15 minutes or until the biscuits are just set. Remove from the oven and leave to cool completely on the baking sheets.

4 Make the icing. Put the chocolate and cream in a bowl set over a pan of gently simmering water. Heat gently, stirring, until the chocolate is melted. Cool and then chill for 30 minutes. Whip the chocolate mixture until it is thick and fluffy and use it to sandwich the biscuits together to make kisses. Serve with espresso coffee.

Chocolate chip and ginger cookies

Preparation time **10 minutes**
Cooking time **10–12 minutes**
Makes **40 cookies**

100 g (3½ oz) unsalted butter,
  softened
100 g (3½ oz) caster sugar
100 g (3½ oz) light soft brown sugar
2 eggs, lightly beaten
200 g (7 oz) self-raising flour
100 g (3½ oz) chocolate chips
50 g (2 oz) crystallized ginger, finely
  chopped

1 Put the butter and sugar in a bowl and beat together until the mixture is light and fluffy. Gradually beat in the eggs, a little at a time, beating well after each addition until the mixture becomes creamy. Stir in the flour and fold in the chocolate chips and ginger to make a soft, sticky dough.

2 Drop teaspoonfuls of the mixture, spaced well apart, on to 2 lightly oiled baking sheets and bake in a preheated oven, 190°C (375°F), Gas Mark 5, for 10–12 minutes or until lightly golden. Leave to cool for 2 minutes on the baking sheets, then use a palette knife to transfer the cookies to a wire rack to cool. Repeat with the remaining dough to make 40 cookies.

Triple chunk toastie

Preparation time **2 minutes**
Cooking time **2–3 minutes**
Serves **2**

4 slices of Italian country-style
   bread
75 g (3 oz) milk chocolate, chopped
75 g (3 oz) plain dark chocolate,
   chopped
75 g (3 oz) white chocolate,
   chopped
25 g (1 oz) toasted hazelnuts,
   roughly chopped (optional)

1 Scatter two slices of country-style bread with the chocolate chunks and the hazelnuts (if used) and top with the remaining bread.

2 Toast in a sandwich grill for 2–3 minutes or according to the manufacturer's instructions until the bread is golden and toasted and the chocolate has begun to melt. Serve immediately.

Mousse tartlets

Preparation time **25 minutes**, plus chilling
Cooking time **20 minutes**
Serves **10**

250 g (8 oz) rich shortcrust pastry (thawed if frozen)
175 g (6 oz) plain dark chocolate, broken into squares
2-3 tablespoons water
15 g (½ oz) unsalted butter, diced
1 tablespoon brandy or Cointreau
3 eggs, separated
chocolate shavings (see page 11), to decorate

1 Roll out the pasty and use it to line 8 tartlet tins, 10 cm (4 inches) across. Reroll the trimmings and line 2 more tins. Chill for 15 minutes, line the tart cases with greaseproof or baking paper and baking beans and bake blind in a preheated oven, 200°C (400°F), Gas Mark 6, for 15 minutes. Remove the paper and beans and bake for a further 5 minutes. Leave to cool.

2 Make the filling. Put the chocolate in a heatproof bowl and add the water. Set the bowl over a pan of hot water and leave, stirring occasionally, until the chocolate has completely melted.

3 Remove the bowl from above the water and stir in the butter until it has melted. Add the brandy or Cointreau and stir in the egg yolks.

4 Beat the egg whites in a clean bowl until they are stiff and dry and fold them into the chocolate mixture.

5 Spoon the mousse mixture into the tartlet cases, then transfer them to the refrigerator for 2–3 hours or until set. Sprinkle with the chocolate shavings and serve cold.

Pamperato

Preparation time **40 minutes**, plus soaking
Cooking time **25–30 minutes**
Makes **3 (each serves 4)**

140 g (4½ oz) raisins
2-3 tablespoons brandy
75 g (3 oz) toasted walnuts, chopped
125 g (4 oz) toasted almonds, chopped
40 g (1½ oz) toasted pine nuts, chopped
100 g (3½ oz) plain dark chocolate, grated
75 g (3 oz) chopped candied orange or tangerine peel
2 tablespoons honey
2 tablespoons water
50 g (2 oz) redcurrant jelly
grated nutmeg
grated rind of 1 orange
¼ teaspoon sea salt
black pepper
125 g (4 oz) plain flour
apricot jam, melted
icing sugar, for dusting

1 Soak the raisins in the brandy and a little warm water for 30 minutes, then drain. Combine the raisins, walnuts, almonds, pine nuts, chocolate and candied citrus peel. Melt the honey in the water and add to the mixture.

2 Stir in the redcurrant jelly, nutmeg, orange rind, salt and 6–10 grindings of pepper. Reserve a little flour and mix the rest in, little by little, to form a dough.

3 On a lightly floured surface, shape the dough into 3 discs, each 13 cm (5½ inches) across, incorporating the rest of the flour. Place on a buttered and floured baking sheet and bake in a preheated oven, 180°C (350°F), Gas Mark 4, for 20–25 minutes or until firm.

4 Brush the top of each disk with melted apricot jam and bake for another 5 minutes. Allow the pamperato to cool briefly, then sieve over a little icing sugar. Leave to mellow in an airtight container for 2–3 days.

Delicious desserts

White chocolate cherry tart

Preparation time **30 minutes**,
plus chilling
Cooking time **about 1 hour**
Serves **6–8**

Pastry
175 g (6 oz) plain flour
½ teaspoon ground cinnamon
125 g (4 oz) unsalted butter, diced
25 g (1 oz) caster sugar
2–3 tablespoons iced water

Filling
2 eggs
40 g (1½ oz) caster sugar
150 g (5 oz) white chocolate,
    chopped
300 ml (½ pint) double cream
450 g (1 lb) fresh black or red
    cherries, stoned, or 2 x 425 g
    (14 oz) cans stoned black or red
    cherries, drained
ground cinnamon, for dusting

1 Make the pastry. Sift the flour and cinnamon into a bowl, add the butter and rub it in with the fingertips. Add the sugar and just enough water to mix to a firm dough. Roll out the dough and use it to line a 23 cm (9 inch) loose-based tart tin. Chill for 30 minutes.

2 Line the tart case with greaseproof or baking paper and baking beans. Bake blind in a preheated oven, 200°C (400°F), Gas Mark 6, for 10 minutes. Remove the paper and beans and return to the oven for 5 minutes.

3 Make the filling. Beat together the eggs and sugar. Heat the chocolate and cream in a small bowl over hot water until the chocolate has melted, then pour over the egg mixture, stirring constantly.

4 Arrange the cherries in the flan case. Pour the chocolate mixture over the cherries and bake in a preheated oven, 180°C (350°F), Gas Mark 4, for about 45 minutes or until the chocolate cream is set. Dust with cinnamon and serve warm.

Double soufflé tart

Preparation time **40 minutes**,
  plus chilling
Cooking time **35 minutes**
Serves **6**

Pastry

200 g (7 oz) plain flour
2 tablespoons cocoa powder
50 g (2 oz) caster sugar
125 g (4 oz) butter, diced, plus extra
  for greasing
2-3 tablespoons water

Filling

125 g (4 oz) white chocolate,
  chopped
25 g (1 oz) butter
4 eggs, separated
75 g (3 oz) caster sugar
grated rind of ½ orange
75 g (3 oz) plain dark chocolate,
  chopped

To decorate

icing sugar, for dusting
white chocolate curls (see page 10)
orange rind curls and orange
  segments

1 Make the pastry. Put the flour, cocoa powder and caster sugar in a bowl and rub in the butter until the mixture resembles fine breadcrumbs. Stir in enough water to make a smooth, soft dough. Knead the dough lightly, roll out on a lightly floured surface and use it to line a 23 cm (9 inch) buttered, loose-based tart tin. Trim off the excess pastry, prick the base with a fork and chill for 15 minutes.

2 Line the tart case with greaseproof or baking paper and baking beans. Bake blind in a preheated oven, 190°C (375°F), Gas Mark 5, for 10 minutes. Remove the paper and beans and cook for 5 more minutes.

3 Make the filling. Melt the white chocolate and butter in a large heatproof bowl set above a saucepan of just-boiled water. Whisk together the egg yolks, caster sugar and orange rind in a large bowl until thick and pale, and the whisk leaves a trail when lifted above the mixture. Fold in the melted chocolate and butter.

4 Use a clean whisk to beat the egg whites into stiff, moist-looking peaks. Fold a large spoonful into the white chocolate mixture to loosen it then fold in the remaining egg whites.

5 Sprinkle the pieces of chocolate over the base of the tart case, then cover with the white chocolate mixture. Bake in a preheated oven, 180°C (350°F), Gas Mark 4, for 20 minutes until the filling is well risen, the top feels crusty and there is a slight wobble to the centre. Check after 15 minutes and cover lightly with foil if the filling seems to be browning too quickly. Leave to cool. As the tart cools, the filling will sink slightly.

6 Remove the tart from the tin and transfer to a serving plate. Dust with icing sugar and top with the chocolate and orange curls. Serve cut into wedges, with some orange segments. (See illustration on pages 42–43.)

Rocky road tart

Preparation time **15 minutes**,
   plus chilling
Serves **8**

Base

125 g (4 oz) butter, melted
50 ml (2 oz) honey
300 g (10 oz) ginger or digestive
   biscuits, broken into crumbs

Filling

150 g (5 oz) honey and almond
   chocolate
1 tablespoon melted butter
75 ml (3 fl oz) double cream
450 ml (¾ pint) chocolate ice cream
450 ml (¾ pint) strawberry ice
   cream
450 ml (¾ pint) vanilla ice cream
100 g (3½ oz) mini-marshmallows
50 g (2 oz) pecan nuts, roughly
   chopped
fresh cherries or strawberries,
   to decorate (optional)

1 Mix together the butter, honey and biscuit crumbs
in a bowl and spoon the mixture into a 25 cm (10 inch)
tart tin, pressing it down into the base and up the sides
with the back of a spoon. Chill for 30 minutes.

2 Make the filling. Put the chocolate, butter and cream
into a heatproof bowl above a pan of simmering water
until the mixture is melted and smooth. Leave to one
side to cool.

3 Scoop the ice creams on to the biscuit base,
alternating the flavours as you go. Sprinkle the top with
the marshmallows and pecan nuts. Drizzle the tart with
the chocolate sauce and put it in the freezer for 2 hours.
Decorate with fresh fruit before serving, if liked.

Velvet pie

Preparation time **35 minutes**,
   plus chilling
Cooking time **22 minutes**
Serves **10**

Shortbread
125 g (4 oz) unsalted butter, diced
175 g (6 oz) plain flour
2 teaspoons cocoa powder
25 g (1 oz) caster sugar

Filling
4 teaspoons powdered gelatine
3 tablespoons cold water
125 g (4 oz) caster sugar
3 egg yolks
1 tablespoon cornflour
600 ml (1 pint) milk
2 tablespoons finely ground
   espresso coffee
50 g (2 oz) plain dark chocolate,
   chopped
chocolate shavings (see page 11),
   to decorate

1 Rub the butter into the sifted flour and cocoa powder, add the sugar and mix to a dough. Press it evenly over the base and sides of a deep 20 cm (8 inch) fluted tart tin. Bake for 20 minutes in a preheated oven, 180°C (350°F), Gas Mark 4, then leave to cool.

2 Soak the gelatine in the water. Whisk together the sugar, egg yolks, cornflour and 2 tablespoons milk. Bring the rest of the milk to the boil with the coffee and whisk into the egg mixture.

3 Return the mixture to the saucepan and heat gently, stirring until it thickens. Remove from the heat and beat in the gelatine until dissolved. Add the chocolate and stir until it has melted. Cool slightly then pour the mixture into the tart case. Chill for several hours.

4 Transfer the pie to a plate and scatter generously with chocolate shavings.

Coffee profiteroles with chocolate sauce

Preparation time **20 minutes**
Cooking time **30 minutes**
Serves **4**

Choux pastry
125 ml (4 fl oz) water
50 g (2 oz) chilled unsalted butter
65 g (2½ oz) plain flour, sifted
pinch of salt
2 eggs, lightly beaten

Chocolate sauce
100 g (3½ oz) plain dark chocolate,
   chopped
50 g (2 oz) unsalted butter, diced
1 tablespoon golden syrup

Coffee cream
300 ml (½ pint) double cream
2 tablespoons made espresso coffee,
   cooled
2 tablespoons Kahlua or Tia Maria

1 Make the choux pastry. Put the water and butter in a small saucepan and heat gently until the butter has melted. Bring to the boil, remove the pan from the heat and immediately beat in the flour and salt until evenly combined. Return the pan to a gentle heat and cook, stirring with a wooden spoon, until the mixture comes together and starts to leave the sides of the pan.

2 Remove the pan from the heat and beat in the eggs with a wooden spoon a little at a time, beating well after each addition until the egg is incorporated and the mixture is smooth and shiny.

3 Line a baking sheet with baking paper. Spoon the choux pastry dough into a piping bag fitted with a 2.5 cm (1 inch) plain nozzle and pipe 12 mounds on to the baking sheet, leaving plenty of space between each one. Bake in a preheated oven, 200°C (400°F), Gas Mark 6, for 20 minutes until puffed up and golden. Remove from the oven, cut a small slit in each one and return to the oven for a further 5 minutes to crisp up. Transfer to a wire rack to cool.

4 Make the chocolate sauce. Put the chocolate, butter and syrup in a small bowl set over a pan of gently simmering water and stir until completely melted. Leave to cool slightly.

5 Meanwhile, make the coffee cream. Whip together the cream, coffee and liqueur until stiff. Cut the choux buns almost in half and spoon or pipe the coffee cream into each one. Serve drizzled with the chocolate sauce.

Pear slice

Preparation time **30 minutes**
Cooking time **about 30 minutes**
Serves **6**

150 g (5 oz) plain dark chocolate,
   chopped
2 large ripe pears
2 tablespoons lemon juice
340 g (11½ oz) puff pastry (thawed
   if frozen)
beaten egg, to glaze
icing sugar, for dusting
single cream, to serve

1 Melt the chocolate in a small heatproof bowl. Quarter, core and thinly slice the pears. Put the pear slices in a bowl of water along with the lemon juice.

2 Roll out the pastry on a lightly floured surface to a rectangle 30 x 18 cm (12 x 7 inches), trimming the edges neatly. Use the tip of a sharp knife to make a shallow cut along each side, 1 cm (½ inch) from the pastry edges. Transfer to a lightly oiled baking sheet that has been sprinkled with water.

3 Spread the melted chocolate to within 1 cm (½ inch) of the cut line. Thoroughly drain the pears and arrange the slices in overlapping lines over the chocolate, keeping them just inside the cut line. Mark small indentations on the edges of the pastry with the back edge of the knife.

4 Brush the pastry edges with beaten egg, then bake in a preheated oven, 200°C (400°F), Gas Mark 6, for about 25 minutes or until the pastry is risen and golden. Remove from the oven.

5 Raise the oven temperature to 230°C (450°F), Gas Mark 8. Generously dust the pastry and pears with icing sugar and return to the oven for about 5 minutes until deep golden, watching closely. Leave to cool slightly, then serve warm with single cream.

Chocolate passionfruit roulade

Preparation time **20 minutes**,
   plus cooling
Cooking time **20 minutes**
Serves **8**

175 g (6 oz) plain dark chocolate,
   chopped
5 eggs, separated
125 g (4 oz) caster sugar, plus extra
   to sprinkle
4 passionfruit, halved and
   scooped out
4 tablespoons orange curd
250 ml (8 fl oz) double cream,
   lightly whipped
chocolate curls (see page 10),
   to decorate

1 Melt the chocolate in a small heatproof bowl. Beat together the yolks and sugar for about 3–4 minutes until thickened and pale. Fold in the melted chocolate.

2 Whisk the egg whites in a clean bowl until peaking but not stiff. Fold a quarter of the whisked whites into the chocolate mix to lighten it, then fold in the remainder.

3 Transfer to a lined, lightly oiled Swiss roll tin, 33 x 23 cm (13 x 9 inches). Bake in a preheated oven, 180°C (350°F), Gas Mark 4, for 20 minutes or until risen and just firm.

4 Invert the roulade on to a sheet of greaseproof paper sprinkled with caster sugar and peel away the lining paper. Cover and leave to cool.

5 Mix the passionfruit pulp with the orange curd. Spread the cream over the roulade, spoon over the passionfruit mix, then roll up the roulade. Turn on to a plate, join underneath, and scatter the curls over the top.

Chocolate hazelnut meringue gâteau

Preparation time **30 minutes**,
    plus chilling
Cooking time **1–1¼ hours**
Serves **8–10**

5 eggs, separated
300 g (10 oz) caster sugar
1 tablespoon cornflour
125 g (4 oz) blanched hazelnuts,
    toasted and finely ground
cocoa powder, to dust

Filling
250 g (8 oz) plain dark chocolate,
    chopped
200 ml (7 fl oz) double cream

Chocolate hazelnuts
50 g (2 oz) hazelnuts
50 g (2 oz) plain dark chocolate,
    melted

1 Whisk the egg whites until they are stiff, then gradually whisk in the sugar, a little at a time, until thick and glossy. Fold in the cornflour and ground hazelnuts until evenly incorporated. Transfer the mixture to a large piping bag fitted with a 1 cm (½ inch) plain nozzle.

2 Draw 3 circles, each 23 cm (9 inches) across, on 3 sheets of baking paper. Put them on separate baking sheets. Starting in the centre of each prepared circle, pipe the mixture in a continuous coil, finishing just within the line. Bake in a preheated oven, 150°C (300°F), Gas Mark 2, for 1–1¼ hours or until lightly golden and dried out. Remove from the oven and transfer to a wire rack to cool completely. Peel away the baking paper.

3 Make the filling. Put the chocolate and cream in a bowl set over a pan of gently simmering water and heat, stirring, until the chocolate is melted. Cool and then chill for 1 hour until thickened.

4 Make the chocolate hazelnuts. Using a fork, dip the hazelnuts into the melted chocolate until coated. Leave to set on baking paper.

5 Beat the chocolate filling until it is light and fluffy and use it to sandwich the meringue layers together. Decorate the gâteau with the chocolate hazelnuts and serve dusted with cocoa powder.

Chocolate cheesecake slice

Preparation time **20 minutes**,
   plus chilling
Cooking time **50–60 minutes**
Serves **12–16**

250 g (8 oz) chocolate biscuits
100 g (3½ oz) unsalted butter,
   melted
50 g (2 oz) plain dark chocolate
500 g (1 lb) cream cheese
150 ml (¼ pint) soured cream
3 eggs
125 g (4 oz) caster sugar
1 teaspoon vanilla extract

1 Process the chocolate biscuits in a food processor until the mixture is smooth, then stir them into the melted butter until they are evenly combined. Lightly oil and line a 18 x 25 cm (7 x 10 inch) cake tin with baking paper, allowing the paper to overhang the edges. Spoon the mixture into the prepared tin and spread it flat. Transfer the tin to the refrigerator.

2 Meanwhile, put the chocolate in a bowl set over a pan of gently simmering water and stir until it has melted. Keep warm.

3 Put the cream cheese, cream, eggs, sugar and vanilla extract in a clean bowl and beat together until smooth. Pour into the tin and drizzle over the melted chocolate, using a skewer to create a swirl pattern over the creamed mixture.

4 Bake in a preheated oven, 150°C (300°F), Gas Mark 2, for 50-60 minutes or until the mixture is firm. Remove from the oven, leave to cool and chill for 1 hour. Carefully remove the cheesecake from the tin and cut it into fingers.

Marble cheesecake

Preparation time **20 minutes**, plus chilling

Cooking time **40–45 minutes**

Serves **8–10**

125 g (4 oz) gingersnap biscuits, broken into crumbs
2 tablespoons cocoa powder
40 g (1½ oz) unsalted butter

Filling
400 g (13 oz) cream cheese
150 g (5 oz) caster sugar
3 eggs
2 teaspoons vanilla extract
150 ml (¼ pint) double cream
200 g (7 oz) plain dark chocolate, chopped
single cream, to serve

1 Mix the crushed biscuits with the cocoa powder. Melt the butter and stir in the biscuit mixture. Press the mix into the base of a 20 cm (8 inch) springform cake tin.

2 Make the filling. Beat the cream cheese to soften it, then beat in the sugar, eggs, vanilla extract and cream. Melt the chocolate in a heatproof bowl. Spoon about one-third of the cream cheese mixture into a separate bowl and beat in the chocolate.

3 Put the cream cheese mixture in the tin, then pour in the cream cheese and chocolate mix. Swirl the mixtures together lightly with a knife to marble them.

4 Bake in a preheated oven, 160°C (325°F), Gas Mark 3, for 35–40 minutes or until the centre of the cheesecake feels only just set. Turn off the oven and leave the cheesecake to cool in it before transferring it to the refrigerator. Serve chilled with single cream.

Caramel rice castles

Preparation time **20 minutes**,
plus cooling
Cooking time **about 1 hour**
Serves **6**

150 g (5 oz) pudding rice
450 ml (¾ pint) milk
1 teaspoon vanilla extract
50 g (2 oz) caster sugar
125 g (4 oz) plain dark chocolate,
chopped
3 egg yolks
150 ml (¼ pint) double cream
single cream or vanilla custard, to
serve (optional)

Caramel
175 g (6 oz) granulated sugar
2 tablespoons water

1 Put the rice, milk, vanilla extract and sugar in a heavy-based saucepan and bring to the boil. Reduce the heat, cover and simmer gently, stirring occasionally, for about 20 minutes or until the rice is just tender and most of the liquid is absorbed.

2 Stir in 100 g (3½ oz) chocolate until melted. Whisk the egg yolks with the cream and stir into the rice.

3 Make the caramel. Put the granulated sugar in a small heavy-based saucepan with the water. Heat very gently until the sugar dissolves. Bring to the boil and boil rapidly until the syrup has turned a pale caramel colour. Stir in 2 tablespoons water, taking care because the syrup is likely to splutter, and cook until the caramel has softened again.

4 Pour the caramel into 6 small moulds or ramekins, tilting them so it coats the sides. Spoon in the rice mixture. Place the moulds in a roasting tin and pour in sufficient hot water to come halfway up the sides of the moulds. Bake in a preheated oven, 180°C (350°F), Gas Mark 4, for 20 minutes until the rice feels only just set. Leave to cool.

5 Meanwhile, melt the remaining chocolate and, using a fine nozzle, scribble lines over 6 serving plates. Loosen the edges of the puddings with a knife, then invert the castles on to serving plates. Serve with single cream or custard, if liked.

Frozen and chilled treats

Chocolate and rosemary ice cream

Preparation time **30 minutes**,
 plus freezing
Cooking time **5 minutes**
Serves **4**

600 ml (1 pint) double cream
150 ml ('/4 pint) milk
seeds from 1 vanilla pod
4 rosemary sprigs, bruised, plus
 extra to garnish
5 egg yolks
125 g (4 oz) caster sugar
125 g (4 oz) plain dark chocolate,
 grated

1 Gently heat the cream, milk, vanilla seeds and rosemary sprigs in a saucepan until almost boiling. Remove from the heat and leave to infuse for 10 minutes. Pick out the rosemary sprigs and reserve.

2 Beat the egg yolks and sugar until pale and then carefully beat in the cream mixture. Strain back into the saucepan and heat gently, stirring constantly, until the custard thickens enough to coat the back of a wooden spoon. Do not allow the custard to boil.

3 Remove the custard from the heat and immediately stir in the chocolate, continuing to stir until it is melted. Transfer to a plastic container, add the rosemary sprigs and leave until completely cold. Discard the rosemary.

4 Freeze the ice cream either in an ice-cream maker, following the manufacturer's instructions, or in the freezer, beating the ice cream after an hour or so to break down any ice crystals. Remove from the freezer 15–20 minutes before serving to soften slightly. Garnish with rosemary sprigs.

Sorbet in chocolate cases

Preparation time **25 minutes**,
   plus chilling and freezing
Cooking time **10 minutes**
Serves **6**

250 g (8 oz) light muscovado sugar
150 g (5 oz) cocoa powder
250 g (8 oz) plain dark chocolate,
   chopped
6 tablespoons coffee liqueur
6 tablespoons double cream

1 Put 1 litre (1¾ pints) cold water in a heavy-based saucepan with the sugar and cocoa powder and cook slowly, stirring, until smooth. Reduce the heat to low and cook gently, stirring frequently, until thick and glossy and thickly coating the back of the wooden spoon, rather like a custard. Leave to cool.

2 Turn the mixture into a plastic tub and freeze for about 4 hours or until mushy. Blend until smooth, then return to the freezer for a further 2 hours or until frozen.

3 Make the chocolate cases. Cut out 6 squares, 15 x 15 cm (5 x 5 inches), of nonstick baking paper. Press these into 6 sections of a 12-section muffin tin, securing them to the base with pieces of masking tape and spacing them apart so they are not bunched up.

4 Melt the chocolate and put a generous dessertspoonful into the base of each paper lining, spreading it up the sides with a small spoon and bringing it up to the points of the squares. Make sure the paper is thickly covered with chocolate. Chill for about 30 minutes until brittle.

5 Carefully peel away the paper and return the chocolate cases to the refrigerator. To serve, put small scoops of sorbet in the cases and pour a tablespoon of liqueur and cream over each. (See illustration on pages 60–61.)

Turkish delight and chocolate ripple ice cream

Preparation time **30 minutes**,
  plus freezing
Cooking time **10 minutes**
Serves **6–8**

300 ml (½ pint) milk
4 egg yolks
100 g (3½ oz) caster sugar
1 teaspoon cornflour
300 ml (½ pint) double cream
200 g (7 oz) rose-flavoured Turkish
  delight
100 g (3½ oz) plain dark chocolate,
  chopped
25 g (1 oz) unsalted butter

1 Heat the milk in a heavy-based saucepan until almost boiling. In a bowl beat the egg yolks, 75 g (3 oz) sugar and the cornflour. Add the hot milk, stirring. Return to the pan and cook, stirring with a wooden spoon, until slightly thickened. Turn into a bowl, cover and leave to cool.

2 Whip the cream until it just holds its shape, then stir it into the custard. Freeze in a shallow container for 4–6 hours until softly set, or use an ice-cream maker.

3 Cut up the Turkish delight with scissors and blend in a food processor with 100 ml (3½ fl oz) cold water. Transfer to a small pan and cook gently until smooth and syrupy.

4 Put the chocolate in a pan and add the butter, the rest of the sugar and 2 tablespoons water. Heat the mixture gently to make a smooth sauce.

5 When the sauces are cool but still runny, spoon them over the ice cream and fold in. Refreeze until firm.

Watermelon sorbet with chocolate chips

Preparation time **20 minutes**,
    plus chilling and freezing
Cooking time **5 minutes**
Serves **4–6**

750 g (1½ lb) skinned, cubed
    watermelon
300 g (10 oz) caster sugar
1 cinnamon stick
8 tablespoons lemon juice
pink food colouring (optional)
1 egg white
125 g (4 oz) chocolate chips
dessert biscuits, to serve

1 Remove the seeds from the melon with the tip of a knife. Liquidize the melon in a food processor then, with the machine still running, tip in the sugar and blend for 30 seconds.

2 Pour the melon mixture into a saucepan and add the cinnamon stick. Bring slowly to the boil, stirring, until the sugar has dissolved, then turn down the heat and barely simmer for 1 minute. Remove from the heat, add the lemon juice then leave to cool, adding a few drops of pink food colouring (if used).

3 When the melon mixture is cold, remove the cinnamon stick and chill the mixture in the refrigerator for at least 1 hour or overnight to make freezing easier.

4 Pour the sorbet mixture into a shallow freezer tray and freeze until it is frozen around the edges. Mash the sorbet well with a fork, whisk the egg white until it is stiff, then drop spoonfuls of the sorbet into the egg white, whisking all the time until the mixture becomes thick and foamy. Return the sorbet to the freezer to firm it up, then stir in the chocolate chips when it is almost frozen. Then freeze the sorbet until solid. Alternatively, transfer the mixture to an ice-cream maker and follow the manufacturer's instructions.

5 Leave the sorbet to soften in the refrigerator for 20 minutes before serving it with some dessert biscuits.

Iced chocolate and fig terrine

Preparation time **25 minutes**,
  plus soaking and freezing
Serves **8**

2 tablespoons coffee granules
175 ml (6 fl oz) boiling water
175 g (6 oz) dried figs
600 ml (1 pint) double cream
5 tablespoons Tia Maria or other
  coffee-flavoured liqueur
300 g (10 oz) plain dark chocolate,
  chopped
50 g (2 oz) unsalted butter
chocolate leaves or scribbles, to
  decorate (see pages 11 and 12)

1 Mix the coffee with the measurement water, add the figs and leave to steep for 24 hours.

2 Whip 350 ml (12 fl oz) of the double cream with 2 tablespoons of the coffee-flavoured liqueur until the cream is peaking.

3 Use clingfilm to line the base and sides of a 1 kg (2 lb) loaf tin with drop sides and spread the cream mixture into the base and up the sides of the tin to make a case. Freeze for several hours until firm.

4 Drain the figs, reserving the liquid. Put the liquid in a heatproof bowl with the chocolate and butter and melt over a pan of simmering water. Remove from the heat and add the remaining liqueur. Stir lightly to make a smooth sauce.

5 Whip the remaining double cream until just peaking. Stir in the chocolate sauce and figs and mix carefully until everything is evenly combined. Spoon the mixture into the cream-lined tin and level the surface. Freeze for several hours or overnight until firm. Transfer to the refrigerator about 1 hour before serving.

6 Invert the tin to remove the terrine and peel away the clingfilm. Decorate with plenty of chocolate leaves or scribbles and serve sliced.

Chocolate and hazelnut parfait

Preparation time **20 minutes**,
  plus freezing
Cooking time **5–10 minutes**
Serves **6**

125 g (4 oz) blanched hazelnuts
125 g (4 oz) plain dark chocolate,
  chopped
600 ml (1 pint) double cream
2 eggs, separated
175 g (6 oz) icing sugar
dessert biscuits, to serve

To decorate
chocolate curls (see page 10)
cocoa powder

1 Spread the hazelnuts on a baking sheet and toast in a preheated oven, 160°C (325°F), Gas Mark 3, for 5–10 minutes or until golden. Leave to cool completely then grind very finely.

2 Melt the chocolate. Whisk the cream until it holds its shape, then fold in the nuts. Whisk the egg yolks in a large bowl with 2 tablespoons of the sugar until pale and creamy. Whisk the egg whites in another bowl until they form soft peaks, then add the remaining sugar, spoonful by spoonful, whisking until very thick.

3 Stir the chocolate into the egg-yolk mixture. Fold in the cream, then the meringue mixture. Freeze for 12 hours until firm.

4 Soften the parfait in the refrigerator for 10 minutes before serving. Decorate with chocolate curls and dust with cocoa powder. Serve with dessert biscuits.

Chocolate espresso mousse

Preparation time **20 minutes**
Serves **4**

1 tablespoon ground espresso coffee
100 ml (3½ fl oz) boiling water
100 g (3½ oz) plain dark chocolate,
 chopped
15 g (½ oz) unsalted butter
pinch of ground cinnamon
2 small eggs, separated
15 g (½ oz) caster sugar

To decorate
double cream
cocoa powder, for dusting

1 Put the coffee in a cafetière, pour the measured boiling water on top and leave to brew for a few minutes. Melt the chocolate with the butter and cinnamon in a heatproof bowl placed over a saucepan of gently simmering water.

2 Stir the egg yolks into the chocolate, one at a time. Strain the coffee, then gradually stir it into the chocolate mixture. Remove from the heat.

3 Whisk the egg whites until they form soft peaks, then gradually whisk in the sugar. Fold a large spoonful into the chocolate mixture to loosen it, then add the remainder and fold in gently with a large metal spoon.

4 Pour the mousse into small coffee cups and chill for 4 hours or until set. Top with spoonfuls of cream and a light dusting of cocoa powder.

Chocolate trifle

Preparation time **15 minutes**,
   plus chilling
Serves **4**

100 g (3½ oz) almond biscotti
75 ml (3 fl oz) orange juice
1 tablespoon brandy (optional)
200 g (7 oz) ricotta cheese
150 g (5 oz) Greek yogurt
3 tablespoons icing sugar
few drops of vanilla extract
25 g (1 oz) plain dark chocolate,
   grated
100 g (3½ oz) blueberries

1 Soak the biscotti in the orange juice and brandy
(if used).

2 Meanwhile, beat together the ricotta, yogurt, icing
sugar and vanilla extract until smooth and creamy.

3 Spoon the soaked biscotti into the base of 4 glass
sundae dishes. Divide half the cheese mixture among
the glasses. Top with half the grated chocolate and then
the blueberries. Spoon the remaining cheese mixture
into the dishes and finish with a semicircle of grated
chocolate. Chill for at least 30 minutes before serving.

Peppered panna cotta with strawberry sauce

Preparation time **20 minutes**, plus chilling
Cooking time **3 minutes**
Serves **6**

1 teaspoon pink peppercorns in brine
1 teaspoon powdered gelatine
2 tablespoons water
250 g (8 oz) mascarpone cheese
300 ml (½ pint) double cream
150 g (5 oz) white chocolate, chopped
300 g (10 oz) strawberries
2–3 tablespoons icing sugar

To decorate
piped chocolate scribbles (see page 12)
fresh strawberries

1 Rinse and dry the peppercorns. Use a pestle and mortar to crush them until they are fairly finely ground. Sprinkle the gelatine over the water in a small bowl and leave the mixture to stand for 5 minutes. Lightly oil 6 x 125 ml (4 fl oz) dariole moulds.

2 Put the mascarpone in a medium-sized saucepan with the cream and crushed peppercorns and bring just to the boil, stirring, until smooth. Remove from the heat and add the gelatine. Stir for about 1 minute until dissolved, then tip in the chocolate. Leave until melted.

3 Pour into 6 lightly oiled dariole moulds, each holding 125 ml (4 fl oz), stirring between each pour to distribute the peppercorns evenly. Chill for several hours or overnight until set.

4 Blend the strawberries in a food processor with a little icing sugar and 1 tablespoon water until smooth. Test for sweetness, adding more sugar if necessary.

5 Loosen the edges of the moulds with a knife and shake them out on to plates. Spoon the sauce around and decorate with chocolate scribbles and strawberries.

Zuccotto

Preparation time **15–20 minutes**,
plus chilling
Cooking time **35–40 minutes**
Serves **6–8**

3 large eggs
75 g (3 oz) caster sugar
50 g (2 oz) plain flour
1 tablespoon cocoa powder, plus
extra for dusting
1 tablespoon oil

Filling
4 tablespoons brandy
350 ml (12 fl oz) double cream
40 g (1½ oz) icing sugar, sifted
50 g (2 oz) plain dark chocolate,
chopped
25 g (1 oz) almonds, chopped
and toasted
175 g (6 oz) cherries, pitted
2 tablespoons Kirsch

1 Place the eggs and caster sugar in a bowl and whisk over a saucepan of hot water until thick. Sift the flour and cocoa powder into the bowl and fold in, then fold in the oil. Spoon into a lightly greased 20 cm (8 inch) cake tin and bake in a preheated oven, 180°C (350°F), Gas Mark 4, for 35–40 minutes. Turn on to a wire rack.

2 When it is cool, cut the sponge in half horizontally and line a 1.8 litre (3 pint) bowl with one layer. Sprinkle with brandy. Whip the cream to soft peaks. Fold in 25 g (1 oz) of the icing sugar, the chocolate, almonds, cherries and Kirsch. Spoon into the bowl and top with the remaining sponge. Cover with a plate and chill.

3 Turn the zuccotto out on to a plate. Cut a circle of greaseproof paper to cover the zuccotto, fold it into 8 sections and cut out alternate sections. Position the paper over the zuccotto and sift cocoa powder over. Move the paper round to cover the cocoa powder and sift icing sugar over.

Lime creams

Preparation time **5 minutes**,
plus chilling
Cooking time **2 minutes**
Serves **4**

50 g (2 oz) caster sugar
finely grated rind and juice of
2 limes
2 tablespoons water
300 ml (½ pint) double cream
100 g (3½ oz) plain or milk
chocolate, coarsely grated

1 Heat the sugar in a small saucepan with the lime rind and juice and the water until the sugar has dissolved. Cool slightly.

2 Put the lime syrup into a bowl with the cream and whisk until softly peaking. Reserve a little of the grated chocolate and fold the remainder into the cream. Spoon the mixture into serving glasses. Serve chilled, sprinkled with the reserved grated chocolate.

Chocolate Amaretto jellies

Preparation time **15 minutes**,
   plus setting
Cooking time **5 minutes**
Serves **8**

1 tablespoon powdered gelatine
3 tablespoons water
300 g (10 oz) plain dark chocolate,
   chopped
150 ml (¼ pint) Amaretto liqueur
450 ml (¾ pint) milk
100 ml (3½ fl oz) double cream
1 quantity Glossy Chocolate Sauce
   (see page 14)

1 Sprinkle the gelatine over the water in a small bowl and leave to soak for 5 minutes. Melt the chocolate in a large bowl with the liqueur, stirring frequently, until the mixture is smooth.

2 Bring the milk just to the boil and remove from the heat. Pour the warm milk over the chocolate, whisking well until completely smooth.

3 Add the soaked gelatine and stir for 1 minute until dissolved. Divide among 8 individual moulds, each 125–150 ml (4–5 fl oz), and leave to cool. Chill for at least 6 hours, preferably overnight, until just firm.

4 Half-fill a small bowl with very hot water and dip a mould up to the rim in the water for 2 seconds. Invert on to a serving plate and, gripping both plate and mould, shake the jelly out on the plate. Lift away the mould and repeat with the other jellies.

5 Pour a little cream around each jelly, then drizzle a tablespoonful of sauce through it. Lightly swirl the syrup into the cream to decorate.

Triple chocolate brûlée

Preparation time **30 minutes**,
   plus freezing and chilling
Cooking time **5 minutes**
Serves **6**

8 egg yolks
125 g (4 oz) caster sugar
600 ml (1 pint) double cream
125 g (4 oz) plain dark chocolate,
   chopped
125 g (4 oz) white chocolate,
   chopped
125 g (4 oz) milk chocolate,
   chopped
3 tablespoons Amaretto di Saronno
   or brandy (optional)
plain, milk and white chocolate
   curls (see page 10), to decorate
   (optional)

1 Use a fork to mix together the egg yolks and 50 g (2 oz) sugar in a bowl. Pour the cream into a saucepan and bring almost to a boil. Gradually beat the cream into the yolk mixture.

2 Strain the custard into a jug, then divide it equally among 3 bowls. Stir a different chocolate into each bowl of hot custard, adding a tablespoon of liqueur (if used). Stir until melted.

3 Spoon the dark chocolate custard into 6 ramekins, allow to cool and then transfer to the freezer for 10 minutes to chill and set.

4 Remove the ramekins from the freezer, stir the white chocolate custard, and spoon it over the dark layer in the dishes. Return to the freezer for 10 minutes.

5 Take the ramekins out of the freezer, stir the milk chocolate custard, and spoon it into the ramekins. Chill the custards in the refrigerator for 3–4 hours or until set. About 25 minutes before serving, sprinkle the tops of the dishes with the remaining sugar and caramelize with a blowtorch. Leave at room temperature until ready to eat, then decorate with chocolate curls, if liked.

White chocolate mint brûlée

Preparation time **30 minutes**,
   plus chilling
Cooking time **25–30 minutes**
Serves **6**

600 ml (1 pint) double cream
200 g (7 oz) white chocolate,
   chopped
6 egg yolks
50 g (2 oz) caster sugar
50 g (2 oz) strong, hard white
   peppermints, crushed
3 tablespoons icing sugar,
   to decorate

1 Pour the cream into a saucepan and bring just to a boil. Remove from the heat and add the chocolate. Allow to stand for 5 minutes until melted, stirring occasionally.

2 Mix the egg yolks and sugar in a bowl with a fork. Gradually mix in the chocolate cream, then strain it back into the saucepan. Stir in the crushed peppermints.

3 Put the custard in 6 ramekins or custard cups arranged in a roasting tin. Fill the tin to halfway up the sides of the dishes with warm water. Bake in a preheated oven, 180°C (350°F), Gas Mark 4, for 20–25 minutes or until the custard is set with a slight softness at the centre.

4 Leave the dishes to cool in the water, then lift them out and chill in the refrigerator for 3–4 hours. About 20–30 minutes before serving, sprinkle the sugar over the top of the desserts. Caramelize with a blowtorch and leave at room temperature until ready to serve.

Hot puddings

Steamed chocolate pudding with date and orange sauce

Preparation time **20 minutes**
Cooking time **1¾ hours**
Serves **6**

75 g (3 oz) unsalted butter, softened
150 g (5 oz) light muscovado sugar
finely grated rind of 1 orange
2 eggs
150 g (5 oz) self-raising flour
25 g (1 oz) cocoa powder
½ teaspoon bicarbonate of soda
100 g (3½ oz) milk chocolate,
    chopped
single cream or custard, to serve

Sauce
125 g (4 oz) light muscovado sugar
75 g (3 oz) unsalted butter
4 tablespoons orange juice
50 g (2 oz) stoned dates, chopped

1 Put the butter, sugar, orange rind and eggs in a large bowl. Sift the flour, cocoa powder and bicarbonate of soda into the bowl and beat well until light and creamy. Stir in the chocolate.

2 Lightly butter and base-line a 1.2 litre (2 pint) pudding basin, turn the mixture into the basin and level the surface. Cover with a double thickness of greaseproof paper and a sheet of foil, securing them under the rim of the basin with string.

3 Bring a 5 cm (2 inch) depth of water to the boil in a large saucepan. Lower in the pudding and cover with a lid. Steam for 1¾ hours, topping up the water occasionally if necessary.

4 Meanwhile, make the sauce. Put the sugar, butter and orange juice in a small saucepan and heat gently until the sugar dissolves. Bring to the boil and boil for 1 minute. Stir in the dates and cook for 1 minute.

5 Invert the pudding on to a serving plate and pour the sauce over the top. Serve with single cream or custard.

Bread and butter pudding

Preparation time **15 minutes**,
  plus standing
Cooking time **about 50 minutes**
Serves **6**

200 g (7 oz) plain dark chocolate,
  chopped
50 g (2 oz) unsalted butter
½ teaspoon ground mixed spice
250 g (8 oz) brioche
3 eggs
25 g (1 oz) caster sugar
600 ml (1 pint) milk
cocoa powder or icing sugar,
  for dusting

1 Put the chocolate in a heatproof bowl with 25 g (1 oz) butter and the mixed spice. Place over a pan of simmering water and leave until melted. Stir the ingredients together.

2 Lightly grease a shallow, 1.8 litre (3 pint) ovenproof dish. Cut the brioche into thin slices and arrange about a third of the slices in the dish.

3 Pour spoonfuls of the chocolate sauce over the bread. Cover with another third of the bread and then the remaining sauce. Arrange the rest of the bread on top.

4 Melt the remaining butter and beat it together with the eggs, sugar and milk. Pour the mixture over the bread and leave to stand for 30 minutes.

5 Bake in a preheated oven, 180°C (350°F), Gas Mark 4, for about 50 minutes until the crust is golden. Serve the pudding liberally dusted with cocoa powder or icing sugar.

Sunken torte with orange liqueur

Preparation time **20 minutes**
Cooking time **30 minutes**
Serves **8**

250 g (8 oz) plain dark chocolate,
   chopped
125 g (4 oz) unsalted butter
1 teaspoon vanilla extract
6 medium eggs, separated
125 g (4 oz) light muscovado sugar
250 ml (8 fl oz) Greek yogurt
finely grated rind and juice of
   ½ orange
2 tablespoons orange liqueur
2 tablespoons icing sugar
chocolate curls (see page 10),
   to decorate

1 Melt the chocolate with the butter and stir in the vanilla extract. Whisk the egg yolks with 100 g (3½ oz) sugar for 3–4 minutes until the mixture leaves a trail when the whisk is lifted. Fold in the chocolate mixture.

2 Whisk the egg whites in a clean bowl until peaking. Gradually whisk in the remaining sugar. Fold a quarter of the whisked whites into the chocolate mixture to lighten it, then fold in the remainder.

3 Grease and base-line a 23 cm (9 inch) springform cake tin, then grease the paper. Turn the mixture into the tin and bake in a preheated oven, 160°C (325°F), Gas Mark 3, for 30 minutes or until well risen and springy.

4 Beat together the yogurt, orange rind and juice, liqueur and icing sugar until smooth, then chill. Allow the cake to cool in the tin for 10 minutes before serving with the orange cream and chocolate curls.

Chocolate fig tatin

Preparation time **20 minutes**
Cooking time **35 minutes**
Serves **6**

100 g (3½ oz) plain dark chocolate,
    grated
1 teaspoon ground mixed spice
75 g (3 oz) caster sugar, plus
    2 tablespoons
500 g (1 lb) puff pastry (thawed
    if frozen)
75 g (3 oz) unsalted butter, plus
    extra for greasing
10 fresh figs, quartered
1 tablespoon lemon juice
vanilla ice cream or crème fraîche,
    to serve

1 Mix together the grated chocolate, spice and
2 tablespoons sugar. Cut the pastry into 3 evenly sized
pieces and roll out each to a circle 25 cm (10 inches)
across, using a plate or inverted bowl as a guide.

2 Scatter 2 rounds to within 2 cm (¾ inch) of the edges
with the grated chocolate mixture. Stack the pastry
layers so that the chocolate is sandwiched in 2 layers.
Press the pastry down firmly around the edges.

3 Lightly butter the sides of a round, shallow, 23 cm
(9 inch) baking tin, 4 cm (1½ inches) deep. (Don't use
a loose-based tin.) Melt the butter in a frying pan. Add
the sugar and heat gently until dissolved. Add the figs
and cook for 3 minutes or until lightly coloured and the
syrup begins to turn golden. Add the lemon juice.

4 Tip the figs into the tin, spreading them in an even
layer. Lay the pastry over the figs, tucking the dough
down inside the edges of the tin. Bake in a preheated
oven, 200°C (400°F), Gas Mark 6, for 30 minutes until
well risen and golden. Leave for 5 minutes, then loosen
the edges and invert on to a serving plate. Serve with
ice cream or crème fraîche.

Risotto

Preparation time **20 minutes**
Cooking time **40 minutes**
Serves **4**

600 ml (1 pint) milk
25 g (1 oz) sugar
50 g (2 oz) butter
125 g (4 oz) arborio rice
50 g (2 oz) hazelnuts, toasted and
  chopped
50 g (2 oz) sultanas
125 g (4 oz) plain dark chocolate,
  grated
splash of brandy (optional)
grated chocolate, to decorate

1 Put the milk and sugar into a saucepan and heat until almost boiling.

2 Melt the butter in a heavy-based saucepan, add the rice and stir well to coat the grains.

3 Add the hot milk, a ladleful at a time, stirring until each addition is absorbed into the rice. Continue adding milk in this way, cooking until the rice is creamy but the grains are still firm. This should take 25–35 minutes.

4 Finally, add the hazelnuts, sultanas, grated chocolate and a splash of brandy (if used) and mix quickly. Serve immediately, decorated with grated chocolate.

Chocolate fudge fondue

Preparation time **15 minutes**
Cooking time **10 minutes**
Serves **6**

150 g (5 oz) light muscovado sugar
50 g (2 oz) unsalted butter
200 g (7 oz) plain dark chocolate,
    chopped
1 teaspoon vanilla extract
100 ml (3½ fl oz) soured cream

To serve
2 bananas
200 g (7 oz) sweet raisin bread
handful of strawberries and cherries

1 Put the sugar in a saucepan with 100 ml (3½ fl oz) water. Heat gently until the sugar dissolves, then bring to the boil and boil rapidly for about 4 minutes until the syrup is bubbling vigorously and looks dark and treacly.

2 Remove the saucepan from the heat and immerse the base in cold water to prevent further cooking. Add 2 tablespoons water. Return the saucepan to the heat and cook, stirring, until the syrup is smooth and glossy.

3 Add the butter, chocolate and vanilla extract and leave until melted, stirring frequently until the mixture is completely smooth. Stir in the cream and leave to stand while you prepare the dippers.

4 Cut the bananas into chunky pieces and the bread into bite-sized chunks. Reheat the sauce until it is warm but not piping hot, then pour it into small serving cups. Arrange the fruit and bread around the cups to serve.

White chocolate soufflé

Preparation time **30 minutes**
Cooking time **15–20 minutes**
Serves **4**

butter, for greasing
75 g (3 oz) caster sugar, plus 4
   teaspoons for lining the dishes
3 egg yolks
40 g (1½ oz) plain flour
250 ml (8 fl oz) milk
175 g (6 oz) white chocolate,
   chopped
1 teaspoon vanilla extract
5 egg whites
sifted drinking chocolate powder
   and icing sugar, for dusting

Chocolate sauce
150 g (5 oz) plain dark chocolate,
   chopped
125 ml (4 fl oz) milk
4 tablespoons double cream
25 g (1 oz) caster sugar

1 Lightly butter 4 soufflé dishes, each about 10 cm (4 inches) across and 6 cm (2½ inches) deep. Sprinkle 1 teaspoon caster sugar over the buttered surface to line each dish with sugar. Stand the dishes on a baking sheet.

2 Whisk half the remaining caster sugar and the egg yolks in a bowl until thick, pale and mousse-like. Sift the flour over the surface and gently fold it in.

3 Bring the milk just to the boil in a saucepan, then gradually whisk it into the egg mixture. Return the milk mixture to the pan and cook, stirring continuously, over a medium heat until the mixture is thickened and smooth. Remove the pan from the heat, add half the white chocolate and stir until melted. Mix in the vanilla extract, cover and leave to cool.

4 Whisk the egg whites into stiff, moist-looking peaks. Gradually whisk in the remaining caster sugar, a teaspoon at a time, until thick and glossy. Fold a large spoonful of egg whites into the cooled sauce to loosen the mixture, then fold in the remaining white chocolate. Gently fold in the remaining egg whites.

5 Spoon the mixture into the prepared soufflé dishes and bake in a preheated oven, 220°C (425°F), Gas Mark 7, for 10–12 minutes or until the soufflés are well risen and browned on top and there is a slight wobble to the the soufflé centres.

6 Meanwhile, gently heat all the sauce ingredients together in a small, heavy-based saucepan, stirring until smooth, then pour into a serving jug. Dust the tops of the soufflés with sifted drinking chocolate powder and icing sugar and serve immediately, with some of the warmed sauce drizzled over each one.

Cakes, teabreads
and loaves

Chocolate truffle cake

Preparation time **15 minutes**
Cooking time **35 minutes**
Serves **8**

250 g (8 oz) plain dark chocolate,
     chopped
125 g (4 oz) unsalted butter
50 ml (2 fl oz) double cream
4 eggs, separated
125 g (4 oz) caster sugar
2 tablespoons cocoa powder, sifted
icing sugar, for dusting

To serve
whipped cream
strawberries

1 Melt together the chocolate, butter and cream in a bowl set over a pan of gently simmering water until completely melted. Remove from the heat and leave the mixture to cool for 5 minutes.

2 Whisk the egg yolks with 75 g (3 oz) sugar until pale and then stir in the cooled chocolate mixture.

3 Whisk the egg whites in a clean bowl until soft peaks form and then whisk in the remaining sugar. Fold into the egg mixture with the sifted cocoa powder until evenly incorporated.

4 Lightly oil and base-line a 23 cm (9 inch) springform cake tin and lightly dust it all over with a little extra cocoa powder. Pour the cake mix into the prepared tin and bake in a preheated oven, 180°C (350°F), Gas Mark 4, for 35 minutes. Leave the cake to cool in the tin for 10 minutes, then turn out on to a serving plate. Dust the cake with icing sugar and serve in wedges with whipped cream and strawberries.

Fudge and coconut cake

Preparation time **45 minutes**,
plus cooling
Cooking time **about 25 minutes**
Serves **12–14**

175 g (6 oz) unsalted butter
175 g (6 oz) caster sugar
150 g (5 oz) plain flour
1 teaspoon baking powder
3 eggs
125 g (4 oz) desiccated coconut
2 teaspoons vanilla extract
3 tablespoons milk

Filling
175 g (6 oz) plain dark chocolate,
chopped
75 g (3 oz) unsalted butter
150 g (5 oz) icing sugar
2 tablespoons milk

To decorate
200 g (7 oz) plain dark chocolate,
chopped
25 g (1 oz) unsalted butter
chocolate curls (see page 10)
toasted coconut curls
cocoa powder, for dusting

1 Cream together the butter and sugar until softened. Sift the flour and baking powder into the bowl. Add the eggs, coconut, vanilla extract and milk and beat together until light and creamy.

2 Grease and base-line 2 round, 20 cm (8 inch) sandwich tins. Turn the cake mixture into the tins and level the surfaces. Bake in a preheated oven, 180°C (350°F), Gas Mark 4, for about 25 minutes or until risen and just firm to touch. Transfer to a wire rack to cool.

3 Make the filling. Put the chocolate and butter in a heatproof bowl over a saucepan of simmering water and leave until melted. Remove the bowl from the heat and beat in the icing sugar and milk.

4 Leave the mixture until it is cool enough to form soft peaks. Split each cake horizontally into 2 layers. Place one layer on a plate and spread with a quarter of the filling. Cover with a second layer of sponge and more filling. Repeat the layering, finishing with a layer of sponge so that you have a quarter of the filling left. Spread this around the sides of the cake to fill any gaps.

5 To decorate the cake, put the chocolate and butter in a heatproof bowl over a saucepan of simmering water and leave until melted. Stir the melted chocolate lightly and leave to cool until it thickly coats the back of a spoon. Pour the melted chocolate over the top of the cake, easing it around the sides with a palette knife until completely coated. Decorate the top of the cake with chocolate curls and toasted coconut curls and leave to set. Dust with cocoa powder before serving.

Chocolate mousse cake with frosted blueberries

Preparation time **25 minutes**
Cooking time **about 35 minutes**
Serves **8**

250 g (8 oz) plain dark chocolate, chopped
50 g (2 oz) unsalted butter
2 tablespoons brandy
6 eggs, separated
75 g (3 oz) caster sugar

To decorate
275 g (9 oz) large blueberries
1 tablespoon lightly beaten egg white
50 g (2 oz) caster sugar
chocolate caraque (see page 10) (optional)

1 Put the chocolate and butter in a heatproof bowl over a pan of simmering water until it has melted. Remove from the heat and stir in the brandy.

2 Whisk the egg yolks in a large bowl with 50 g (2 oz) caster sugar until thickened and pale. Stir in the chocolate mixture.

3 Whisk the egg whites in a separate bowl until stiff. Gradually whisk in the remaining sugar. Use a large metal spoon to fold a quarter of the egg whites into the chocolate mixture, then fold in the remainder.

4 Grease and base-line a 23 cm (9 inch) springform cake tin. Turn the cake mixture into the tin and bake in a preheated oven, 160°C (325°F), Gas Mark 3, for 35 minutes or until well risen and beginning to crack on the surface. Leave to cool in the tin.

5 Toss the blueberries in a bowl with the egg white until moistened. Turn them out on to a tray lined with greaseproof paper and spread to a single layer. Scatter with the sugar and leave to dry.

6 Transfer the cake to a serving plate. Pile the frosted blueberries on the cake and decorate with chocolate caraque, if liked.

White chocolate and summer berry cake

Preparation time **40 minutes**,
  plus cooling
Cooking time **25–30 minutes**
Serves **12**

5 eggs
150 g (5 oz) caster sugar
150 g (5 oz) plain flour
75 g (3 oz) white chocolate, grated
50 g (2 oz) unsalted butter, melted
200 g (7 oz) strawberries
200 g (7 oz) raspberries
300 ml (½ pint) double cream
4 tablespoons orange liqueur

White chocolate ganache
300 ml (½ pint) double cream
300 g (10 oz) white chocolate,
  chopped

1 Beat the eggs and sugar in a heatproof bowl over a pan of hot water until the whisk leaves a trail when lifted from the bowl. Remove from the heat and whisk for a further 2 minutes.

2 Sift the flour over the mixture, sprinkle with the chocolate and fold in. Drizzle the melted butter over the mixture and fold in. Grease and base-line 2 round 20 cm (8 inch) sandwich tins and lightly grease the paper. Divide the mixture between the tins and bake in a preheated oven, 180°C (350°F), Gas Mark 4, for 25–30 minutes or until just firm. Transfer to a wire rack to cool.

3 Meanwhile, make the ganache. Heat half the cream in a heavy-based saucepan until it is bubbling around the edges. Remove from the heat and stir in the chocolate. Leave to stand until the chocolate has melted. Turn the mixture into a bowl and chill for about 15 minutes until cold. Stir in the remaining cream and whisk until the ganache just holds its shape.

4 Reserve a handful of the fruits and lightly mash the remainder. Whip the cream until it is just peaking. Halve each cake and drizzle with the liqueur. Spread one layer with a third of the whipped cream and then a third of the fruits. Repeat, finishing with a cake layer.

5 Spread a little ganache over the cake to seal in any crumbs, then swirl over the remainder. Scatter with the reserved fruits.

Devil's food cake

Preparation time **20 minutes**
Cooking time **30 minutes**
Serves **8**

125 g (4 oz) plain dark chocolate,
   chopped
150 g (5 oz) unsalted butter
125 g (4 oz) dark brown sugar
1 tablespoon golden syrup
200 g (7 oz) plain flour
15 g (½ oz) cocoa powder, plus extra
   for dusting
1 teaspoon bicarbonate of soda
2 eggs, beaten
125 ml (4 fl oz) milk

Icing
250 g (8 oz) granulated sugar
125 ml (4 fl oz) water
1 egg white
a few drops of vanilla extract or
   1 teaspoon coffee essence or
   1 teaspoon lemon juice

1 Heat the chocolate, butter, sugar and syrup in a heavy-based saucepan until they have just melted.

2 Sift the flour, cocoa powder and bicarbonate of soda into a bowl. Make a well in the centre and stir in the cooled melted ingredients. Stir in the eggs and beat well, then mix in the milk.

3 Base-line and grease a deep, straight-sided 20 cm (8 inch) cake tin and pour the mixture into the tin. Bake in a preheated oven, 180°C (350°F), Gas Mark 4, for 30 minutes or until set. Allow the cake to cool in the tin before turning it out on to a wire rack to cool.

4 Meanwhile, make the icing. Put the sugar and measured water in a heavy-based pan over a low heat and dissolve the sugar without stirring. Bring to the boil and continue boiling, without stirring, until a sugar thermometer registers 114°C (240°F). Just before this temperature is reached, whisk the egg white in a clean, dry bowl until stiff. Remove the syrup from the heat and when the bubbles have subsided, pour the syrup in a thin stream on to the egg white, whisking continuously. When it is thick and opaque, add your chosen flavouring.

5 Coat the top and sides of the cake with the icing, swirling it with a palette knife and working quickly before it sets. When the icing has set, lightly dust the top of the cake with a little cocoa powder.

Chocolate marble cake

Preparation time **20 minutes**
Cooking time **45–50 minutes**
Serves **8**

250 g (8 oz) unsalted butter,
  softened
175 g (6 oz) caster sugar
4 eggs, lightly beaten
225 g (7½ oz) self-raising flour
1 teaspoon baking powder
pinch of salt
50 g (2 oz) ground almonds
125 g (4 oz) dark chocolate
125 g (4 oz) white chocolate

1 Put the butter, sugar, eggs, flour, baking powder, salt and ground almonds in a bowl and whisk together until they are combined. Spoon half the mixture into a bowl.

2 Meanwhile, put the dark and white chocolate into separate bowls and put each one over a pan of gently simmering water. Stir until the chocolate has melted.

3 Reserving 2 tablespoons of each melted chocolate for decoration, stir the remaining dark chocolate into half the cake mix and the remaining white chocolate into the remaining cake mix, folding until evenly combined. Spoon both mixtures alternately into a lightly greased 23 cm (9 inch) kugelhopf tin and use a skewer to swirl the mixture gently to create a marbled effect.

4 Bake in a preheated oven, 180°C (350°F), Gas Mark 4, for 45–50 minutes until a skewer inserted in the centre comes out clean. Cover the cake with foil if it is getting too browned. Remove the cake from the oven, leave to cool in the tin for 10 minutes, then turn it out on to a wire rack to cool.

5 Take the reserved dark and white chocolate and warm each through by immersing the bowls into hot water, stirring until melted. Use teaspoons to drizzle the chocolate over the cake and serve in slices.

Drambuie fruit cake

Preparation time **25 minutes**,
plus soaking
Cooking time **1½ hours**
Serves **16**

300 g (10 oz) sultanas
8 tablespoons Drambuie
250 g (8 oz) unsalted butter,
softened
200 g (7 oz) light muscovado sugar
75 g (3 oz) stem ginger, finely
chopped
4 eggs
200 g (7 oz) plain flour
25 g (1 oz) cocoa powder
1 teaspoon baking powder
175 g (6 oz) unblanched hazelnuts,
roughly chopped
125 g (4 oz) plain dark chocolate,
chopped
125 g (4 oz) milk chocolate,
chopped

1 Put the sultanas and Drambuie in a bowl. Cover and leave for at least 4 hours or overnight.

2 Cream together the butter, sugar and ginger. Gradually beat in the eggs, adding a little of the flour to prevent curdling. Sift the remaining flour into the bowl with the cocoa powder and baking powder. Reserve 25 g (1 oz) of the nuts and 25 g (1 oz) of each type of chopped chocolate and add the remainder with the sultanas and any soaking juices. Stir well until combined.

3 Grease and line a round 20 cm (8 inch) cake tin. Spoon the mixture into the tin and level the surface. Scatter with the reserved chocolate and nuts and bake in a preheated oven, 150°C (300°F), Gas Mark 2, for about 1½ hours or until firm and a skewer inserted into the centre comes out clean. Leave to cool in the tin.

Chocolate and banana teabread

Preparation time **20 minutes**
Cooking time **about 1 hour**
Makes **10 slices**

200 g (7 oz) plain dark chocolate,
  chopped
½ teaspoon ground ginger
200 g (7 oz) unsalted butter,
  softened
2 ripe bananas
175 g (6 oz) caster sugar
3 eggs
250 g (8 oz) self-raising flour
½ teaspoon baking powder
50 g (2 oz) plain dark chocolate,
  chopped, to decorate
icing sugar, for dusting (optional)

1 Put the chocolate in a heatproof bowl with the ginger and 25 g (1 oz) butter. Leave over a saucepan of simmering water until melted.

2 Mash the bananas. Put the remaining butter in a bowl with the sugar and beat until creamy. Add all the eggs and the banana purée to the bowl, sift in the flour and baking powder and beat together until smooth.

3 Lightly grease the base and long sides of a 1 kg (2 lb) loaf tin. Spread a quarter of the creamed mixture into the tin, then spoon over a third of the chocolate mixture. Spread with another quarter of the cake mixture, then more chocolate. Repeat the layering, finishing with a layer of the cake mixture.

4 Scatter the chopped chocolate down the centre of the cake and bake in a preheated oven, 180°C (350°F), Gas Mark 4, for about 1 hour or until a skewer inserted into the centre comes out clean. Leave in the tin for 10 minutes before transferring to a wire rack to cool completely. Dust with icing sugar, if liked.

Bûche de Noël

Preparation time **45 minutes**
Cooking time **25–30 minutes**
Serves **8**

4 eggs
125 g (4 oz) caster sugar, plus extra
    for dusting
65 g (2½ oz) plain flour
1 tablespoon cocoa powder
25 g (1 oz) butter, melted and
    cooled

Filling
150 ml (¼ pint) double cream
1 tablespoon milk
250 g (8 oz) can sweetened
    chestnut purée

Crème au beurre au chocolat
75 g (3 oz) caster sugar
4 tablespoons water
2 egg yolks
125–175 g (4–6 oz) unsalted butter
50 g (2 oz) plain dark chocolate,
    chopped

To decorate
icing sugar, sifted
cocoa powder, sifted
holly leaves

1 Whisk the eggs and sugar in a bowl until the mixture is thick and pale and the whisk leaves a heavy trail when lifted. Sift the flour and cocoa together twice and fold into the mixture, followed by the cooled runny butter.

2 Line a 30 x 25 cm (12 x 10 inch) Swiss roll tin and grease the paper. Turn the mixture into the tin, spreading it into the corners. Bake in a preheated oven, 190°C (375°F), Gas Mark 5, for 15-20 minutes or until just firm and springy to the touch.

3 Turn out the cake on a sheet of greaseproof paper or nonstick baking paper dredged with caster sugar. Peel off the lining paper, trim the edges of the cake with a sharp knife, then roll up the cake with the sugared paper inside. Leave to cool on a wire rack.

4 Meanwhile, whip together the cream and milk until stiff, then fold the mixture into the chestnut purée. Carefully unroll the cake, remove the paper and spread it evenly with the chestnut mixture. Reroll the cake.

5 Make the crème au beurre au chocolat. Heat the sugar and measurement water in a heavy-based saucepan until dissolved. Bring to the boil and boil steadily for 3–4 minutes until the temperature reaches 110°C (225°F) or the syrup forms a thin thread. Pour the syrup in a thin stream on to the egg yolks, whisking until the mixture is thick and cold. Beat the butter until soft and gradually beat in the egg mixture. Melt the chocolate with 1 tablespoon water over a saucepan of hot water, stirring continuously. Cool, then beat into the syrup mixture.

6 Coat the cake with the chocolate mixture. Use a palette knife to make marks that look like tree bark. Chill until set. Before serving, dust lightly with cocoa powder and icing sugar and decorate with holly leaves. (See illustration on pages 92–93.)

Chocolate mini loaves

Preparation time **20 minutes**,
   plus proving
Cooking time **15 minutes**
Makes **6 loaves**

250 g (8 oz) strong white flour
½ teaspoon salt
2 tablespoons caster sugar
¾ teaspoon fast-action dried yeast
25 g (1 oz) unsalted butter, diced
2 eggs, beaten
3 tablespoons lukewarm milk
50 g (2 oz) plain dark chocolate

To decorate
cocoa powder
icing sugar

1 Put the flour in a large bowl. Stir in the salt, sugar and yeast and rub in the butter with your fingertips until the mixture resembles fine breadcrumbs. Add the eggs and enough warm milk to make a soft dough.

2 Knead well on a lightly floured surface for 5 minutes until the dough is smooth and elastic. Put the dough back into the bowl, cover loosely with oiled clingfilm and leave in a warm place to rise for 1 hour or until it has doubled in size.

3 Tip out the dough on to a lightly floured surface, knead well then cut into 6 pieces. Cut the chocolate into 6 pieces. Roll 1 piece of dough at a time to a rectangle 7 x 10 cm (3 x 4 inches), add a piece of the chocolate then wrap the dough around it and transfer to a greased 10 x 5.5 x 3.5 cm (4 x 2¼ x 1½ inch) mini loaf tin. Repeat to fill 6 tins.

4 Put the loaf tins on a baking sheet, cover the tops loosely with oiled clingfilm and leave in a warm place for 40 minutes until they are well risen and the dough reaches just above the tops of the tins.

5 Remove the clingfilm, bake in a preheated oven, 200°C (400°F), Gas Mark 6, for 12–15 minutes until the breads are well risen and golden and sound hollow when tapped with the fingertips. Carefully loosen the edges of the breads with a small palette knife and transfer to a wire rack to cool. Decorate with a little sifted cocoa and icing sugar.

Chocolate pecan spiral

Preparation time **20 minutes**,
  plus proving
Cooking time **35–40 minutes**
Makes **1 loaf**

500 g (1 lb) strong white flour
40 g (1½ oz) unsalted butter, diced
½ teaspoon salt
50 g (2 oz) caster sugar
1½ teaspoon fast-action dried yeast
2 eggs, beaten
175 ml (6 fl oz) lukewarm milk

Filling
125 g (4 oz) plain dark chocolate,
  finely chopped
125 g (4 oz) pecan nuts, roughly
  chopped
2 tablespoons caster sugar
1 egg yolk, to glaze

1 Put the flour in a large bowl, add the butter and rub it in with your fingertips until the mixture resembles fine breadcrumbs. Stir in the salt, sugar and yeast. Then add the eggs and gradually mix in enough warm milk to make a soft dough.

2 Knead well on a lightly floured surface for 5 minutes until the dough is smooth and elastic. Put the dough back into the bowl, cover loosely with oiled clingfilm and leave in a warm place to rise for 1 hour or until it has doubled in size.

3 Tip the dough on to a lightly floured surface, knead well and then roll it out to a 27 cm (11 inch) square. Sprinkle with three-quarters of the chocolate and nuts and all the sugar.

4 Roll up the dough then put it into a greased 1.5 kg (3 lb) loaf tin. Cover loosely with oiled clingfilm and leave in a warm place for 30 minutes or until the dough reaches just above the top of the tin.

5 Remove the clingfilm, brush with the egg yolk mixed with 1 tablespoon of water and sprinkle with the remaining chocolate and pecan nuts. Bake in a preheated oven, 200°C (400°F), Gas Mark 6, for 35–40 minutes or until the bread is well risen and deep brown and sounds hollow when tapped with the fingertips. Cover with foil after 10 minutes to prevent the nuts from browning. Carefully remove from the tin and transfer to a wire rack to cool.

Sweet things and drinks

Fruit and nut discs

Preparation time **10 minutes**,
  plus setting
Makes **18 sweets**

100 g (3½ oz) plain dark chocolate,
  chopped
100 g (3½ oz) milk chocolate,
  chopped
100 g (3½ oz) white chocolate,
  chopped
125 g (4 oz) dried tropical fruit
  medley, such as pineapple,
  mango, papaya and melon
25 g (1 oz) blanched almonds
25 g (1 oz) unblanched hazelnuts

1 Melt all the chocolate in separate bowls. Spoon it on to 3 separate sheets of nonstick baking paper and spread it out to 16 x 12 cm (6½ x 5 inch) rectangles.

2 Use a 5 cm (2 inch) round metal biscuit cutter to make 6 impressions in each chocolate rectangle to mark the edges of each disc.

3 Cut the dried fruits into small, flattish pieces and arrange them within the marked discs together with the nuts. Chill or leave in a cool place until the chocolate is set but not brittle.

4 Use the cutter to cut out the discs and carefully lift them from the paper. Store in a cool place.

Chocolate ginger clusters

Preparation time **20 minutes**, plus chilling
Makes **20–25 clusters**

175 g (6 oz) white chocolate, chopped
50 g (2 oz) crystallized ginger, chopped
100 g (3½ oz) blanched almonds, lightly toasted and chopped
175 g (6 oz) plain dark chocolate, chopped

1 Put the white chocolate in a heatproof bowl and leave over a saucepan of simmering water until the chocolate has melted.

2 Stir the crystallized ginger and the nuts into the melted chocolate. Place teaspoonfuls of the mixture on a baking sheet lined with greaseproof paper and chill until the mixture is firm.

3 Put the plain chocolate in a heatproof bowl over a saucepan of simmering water and leave until the chocolate has melted.

4 Pierce each cluster with a thin skewer or wooden cocktail stick and dip into the melted chocolate, allowing any excess to drip back into the bowl. Place on a clean sheet of greaseproof paper to set.

Chocolate rum truffles

Preparation time **30 minutes**,
  plus cooling and chilling
Cooking time **10 minutes**
Makes about **16 truffles**

75 g (3 oz) plain dark chocolate,
  chopped
25 g (1 oz) unsalted butter
125 g (4 oz) icing sugar, sifted
2 tablespoons dark rum
cocoa powder

1 Melt the chocolate gently in a bowl over a saucepan of simmering water. Remove the bowl from the heat and leave the chocolate to cool.

2 Beat together the butter and icing sugar until light and fluffy. Add the cooled, melted chocolate and rum and stir until thoroughly combined. Cover and refrigerate until firm.

3 Remove the chocolate mixture from the refrigerator and shape the mixture into 2.5 cm (1 inch) balls. Roll each ball in the cocoa powder and place on a wax paper-lined baking sheet. Refrigerate until firm. Remove the truffles from the refrigerator and leave to stand at room temperature for 30 minutes before serving.

Classic truffles

Preparation time **20 minutes**,
    plus cooling and chilling
Cooking time **5 minutes**
Makes **400 g (13 oz)**

150 ml (¼ pint) double cream
250 g (8 oz) plain dark chocolate,
    finely chopped
25 g (1 oz) unsalted butter, diced
2 tablespoons brandy, rum,
    Cointreau or coffee liqueur
cocoa powder, for dusting

1 Put the cream in a small, heavy-based saucepan and bring it just to the boil. Remove from the heat and tip in the chocolate and butter. Leave until melted, stirring several times until smooth.

2 Turn the mixture into a bowl and add the chosen liqueur. Chill for several hours or overnight until firm.

3 Sprinkle plenty of cocoa powder on a large plate. Take a teaspoonful of the chocolate mixture, roll it lightly in the palm of your hand and coat the ball in the cocoa powder. For more rugged, textured-looking truffles, don't roll them, just sprinkle the spoonfuls of chocolate with the cocoa powder.

4 Arrange the truffles in individual paper cases or pile them on a serving dish. Store in a cool place or in the refrigerator for up to 2 days before serving.

Chocolate mint fudge

Preparation time **15 minutes**,
  plus chilling
Makes **800 g (1 lb 10 oz)**

500 g (1 lb) plain dark chocolate,
  chopped
400 g (13 oz) can sweetened
  condensed milk
40 g (1½ oz) strong peppermints,
  finely crushed
50 g (2 oz) milk or white chocolate,
  melted

1 Put the plain chocolate and condensed milk in a heatproof bowl over a pan of gently simmering water. Leave until melted, stirring frequently. Stir in the ground peppermints and beat to combine thoroughly.

2 Line a shallow 18 cm (7 inch) baking tin with nonstick baking paper. Turn the mixture into the tin, spreading it into the corners. Level the surface and leave to cool. Chill for at least 2 hours.

3 Lift the fudge from the tin and peel away the paper from around the sides. Melt the milk or white chocolate and put it in a paper piping bag. Snip off the tip and scribble lines of chocolate over the fudge. Cut into 2 cm (¾ inch) squares and transfer to a serving plate.

Chocolate and coconut ice

Preparation time **10 minutes**,
  plus freezing
Cooking time **5 minutes**
Serves **4**

750 ml (1¼ pints) milk
100 g (3½ oz) creamed coconut,
  chopped
25 g (1 oz) cocoa powder
100 g (3½ oz) caster sugar
100 g (3½ oz) plain dark chocolate,
  chopped

1 Put 250 ml (8 fl oz) milk in a medium-sized saucepan
with the coconut, cocoa powder and sugar and heat
gently until the coconut and sugar have dissolved. Bring
to the boil and boil for 3 minutes.

2 Remove from the heat and tip in the chocolate. Leave
until the chocolate has melted, stirring frequently, then
leave to cool.

3 Stir in the remaining milk and pour into a shallow
freezer container. Freeze for 4–6 hours or until frozen
around the edges but still slightly slushy in the centre.
Turn into a food processor and blend lightly until evenly
slushy. Serve immediately or return to the freezer and
repeat the process.

Sweet chocolate sushi

Preparation time **40 minutes**,
plus chilling
Cooking time **10 minutes**
Makes **25–30**

1 kiwifruit, skinned
½ small mango, skinned
3 tablespoons tequila or vodka
250 g (8 oz) Japanese sushi rice
400 ml (14 fl oz) can coconut milk
100 g (3½ oz) caster sugar
1 tablespoon white wine vinegar
100 g (3½ oz) plain dark chocolate,
chopped

1 Cut the fruits into 5 mm (¼ inch) thick sticks and mix them with the liqueur.

2 Put the rice in a heavy-based saucepan with the coconut milk, bring to the boil, then simmer very gently for 10 minutes, stirring frequently, until the rice has the consistency of a thick risotto. Add the sugar and vinegar, cover and leave to cool.

3 Melt the chocolate. Draw 3 rectangles, each 24 x 10 cm (9½ x 4 inches), on 3 sheets of nonstick baking paper so that one long side is on the edge of the paper. Spread the chocolate over them.

4 Spoon the cooled rice on to 3 separate sheets of paper, spreading each to 24 x 8 cm (9½ x 3¼ inches) and pressing down very firmly with the back of a wetted spoon. Arrange a thin line of fruit down the centre of each, reserving the juices.

5 Carefully roll up the fruits and rice in the paper, squeezing the edges of the paper tightly together so that the rice is tightly packed. Roll up the rice in the chocolate. (The chocolate edges should just meet.) Chill for 2 hours then remove the paper. Use a serrated knife to cut the sushi into logs. Serve drizzled with the reserved juices.

Hot chocolate

Preparation time **3 minutes**
Cooking time **3 minutes**
Serves **2**

100 g (3½ oz) plain dark chocolate,
  chopped
350 ml (12 fl oz) milk
100 ml (3½ fl oz) whipping cream,
  lightly whipped
grated chocolate, to sprinkle

1 Melt the chocolate in a small bowl. Heat the milk in a small pan until hot but not boiling. Stir a little of the hot milk into the melted chocolate, scraping up the chocolate from around the sides of the bowl, then pour the chocolate milk into the milk pan.

2 Whisk together and pour into large mugs or heatproof glasses. Spoon over the whipped cream and sprinkle with grated chocolate.

Irish chocolate coffee

Preparation time **5 minutes**
Cooking time **2 minutes**
Serves **2**

1 small orange
15 g (½ oz) caster sugar
25 g (1 oz) plain dark chocolate,
    chopped
2 tablespoons Irish whiskey
300 ml (½ pint) freshly made strong
    black coffee
100 ml (3½ fl oz) whipping cream

1 Pare 2 long strips of orange rind and put them in a medium-sized saucepan with the sugar and 125 ml (4 fl oz) water. Heat gently until the sugar dissolves, then bring to the boil. Remove from the heat and stir in the chocolate until melted.

2 Remove the orange strips and add the whiskey and coffee. Pour into 2 tall heatproof glasses.

3 Lightly whip the cream with 2 tablespoons orange juice and spoon over the coffee. Serve immediately.

Decatini

Preparation time **10 minutes**
Serves **1**

ice cubes
2 measures Stolichnaya Razberi
   (raspberry-flavoured vodka)
½ measure Glossy Chocolate Sauce
   (see page 14)
½ measure double cream
1 measure morello cherry purée
chocolate syrup, to decorate

1 Fill a cocktail shaker with ice cubes and add the vodka, chocolate sauce and half the cream. Shake well and strain into a chilled Martini glass.

2 Shake the cherry purée with the rest of the cream in a clean shaker. Slowly pour the cherry liquid on to a spoon that is held in contact with the chocolate liquid in the glass to produce a layering effect. Decorate with a swirl of chocolate syrup.

Chocotini

Preparation time **10 minutes**
Serves **1**

ice cubes
2 measures vodka
1 measure dark crème de cacao
¼ measure sugar syrup
½ measure Glossy Chocolate Sauce
   (see page 14)
cocoa powder, to decorate

1 Fill a cocktail shaker with ice cubes and add the vodka, crème de cacao, sugar syrup and chocolate sauce and shake well.

2 Strain into a chilled Martini glass that has been decorated with cocoa powder around the rim.

Index

Acknowledgements

Executive Editor: Sarah Ford
Editor: Fiona Robertson
Executive Art Editor: Darren Southern
Design: Lisa Tai
Production Controller: Nigel Reed
Picture Library: Sophie Delpech and Taura Riley

Main photography: © Octopus Publishing Group Limited/ Stephen Conroy.
Other photography: © Octopus Publishing Group Limited/ Jean Cazals 41, 74, 92–3, 115; /Gus Filgate 21; /Jeremy Hopley 79; /Graham Kirk 9; /William Lingwood 70; /David Loftus 88; /Lis Parsons 39, 42–3, 71, 80–81, 91; /Gareth Sambidge 6 right, 26; /Simon Smith 35, 100; /Ian Wallace 3, 4, 12, 18–19, 23, 25, 27, 28, 31, 33, 37, 50, 54, 57, 59, 63, 66, 69, 75, 82, 95, 97, 104.